"Finally, a sane book on how to develop healthy self-esteem! Rathe~~~~ ~romoting feeling better than others, this book helps readers to have kindness and con~~~~ for themselves because they are simply human. The sense of unconditional self-worth a~~~~ through the exercises in this book will help transform many lives for the better."

—**Kristin Neff, PhD**, associate professor of human development and cu~~~~ he University of Texas at Austin, and author of *Self-Compassion*

"*The Self-Esteem Workbook* is both excellent and practical because it is built on a sound scientific base, offers clear recommendations, and comes from and speaks to the heart."

—**Steven E. Hobfoll, PhD**, professor and director of the Applied Psychology Center at Kent State University

"Chock-full of effective and practical strategies for raising self-esteem…helpful for anyone who wishes to end negative thinking and learn to see their true value."

—**Matthew McKay, PhD**, coauthor of *Self-Esteem*

"It is impossible to read this book without feeling better about oneself and others. It should be required reading for every living soul."

—**Robert L. Bunnell, MS, PA-C**, marketing coordinator at the University of Utah Physician Assistant Program, and executive director of the Utah Academy of Physician Assistants

"What a wonderful workbook! Even for those of us who feel we have a high level of self-esteem, this book provides insight and techniques for improving those areas that sometimes make us question ourselves and our self worth. With some of my more difficult physical therapy patients, I often employ the cognitive rehearsal technique of acknowledging what is 'right' about themselves to break their negative views of themselves or their situation. This in itself often leads to acceleration in the healing process."

—**Linda C. Harvey, MA, PT**, physical therapy role extender for rehabilitation coordinator for the Visiting Nurses Association of Maryland

"This book is excellent. We are already using it in our self-esteem presentations. It's one of the first and finest self-esteem resource guidebooks that offer in-depth information in a grounded, useful way."

—**Jaqueline Miller**, Maryland Governor's Task Force on Self-Esteem

"Self-esteem—its importance and how to develop and protect it—is a poorly understood concept in today's world of the 'quick fix.' Glenn Schiraldi has done a great service in assembling all of the material on this important topic. His practical, step-by-step format and powerful skill-building exercises lead the participant on a purposeful journey that can result in a future of better mental health and well-being."

—**Sharlene M. Weiss, PhD**, founder and former director of psychosocial oncology at the University of Miami's Sylvester Comprehensive Cancer Center, and associate professor of medicine, psychiatry, and psychology at the University of Miami School of Medicine

"I have been teaching courses in human development for nearly forty years. I am impressed by the wealth of material—activities, exercises, and accompanying narratives—found in Glenn Schiraldi's *The Self-Esteem Workbook*. An excellent resource!"

—**Albert H. Gardner, PhD**, associate professor of human development, and director of Advocates for Children at the University of Maryland

"Dr. Schiraldi has created a hands-on program that can be used as a complete program or for counselors wishing to add specific exercises to treatment. This book is certainly appropriate for continuing education of counselors as well as an office manual. The material is current and well organized."

—**Thomas W. Clawson**, executive director at the National Board for Certified Counselors

"Glenn Schiraldi has skillfully and thoughtfully brought together three essential elements for lasting change: sound principles, practical applications, and a reasonable time frame for real change to occur. It's all right here!"

—**Claudia A. Howard, MEd**, president of Individual Potential Seminars

"It's obvious that this book is a labor of love that was many years in the making. I've gained much by rereading it. It shows that self-esteem can be increased, regardless of one's upbringing, past environment, and experiences. The readings and exercises provide concrete steps to establish the unconditional worth of each human being, cultivate the skill of love, and then help a person to grow and reach out. I particularly enjoyed the inspirational quotes from men and women who have realized their self-worth and thus been able to reach out beyond themselves. This book is a great personal investment!"

—**Pamela G. Barainca, RD, LD**, clinical dietitian

"Even educated people have self-defeating ideas that impair self-esteem. At least one idea from every page has affected myself, my life, and every single person that I have spoken to in my professional life."

—**Mohammad Beiraghdar, MD**

"I found *The Self-Esteem Workbook* to be an infinitely deep wellspring in my work as a volunteer facilitator for groups of victims of abuse. It is clear and easy to understand, and its step-by-step program is perfect for those struggling with self-worth issues. Its timeless content applies to anyone suffering with low self-esteem. I have used it over and over, and will continue to do so. Thank you Glenn Schiraldi!"

—**Janet Harkness**, homemaker and mother

"Brilliant in its simplicity. I have used it extensively as a mental health resource, an invaluable teaching tool, and a gift to close friends."

—**Melissa Hallmark Kerr, PhD**, cofounder of Brain Savvy Leadership

"*The Self-Esteem Workbook* is clearly one of the best written for understanding and exploring the true meaning, importance, and value of building self-esteem. It is a guidebook for healing and loving our inner essential selves. This book encourages us to explore and learn to cherish with awe, the magic that lies within us. A must for teacher training, working with battered and abused populations, and people who are in recovery processes. A terrific workbook. I think every school in America should be working with this information."

—**Sandi Redenbach, MEd**, former chairperson of the California Council to Promote Self-Esteem and Personal and Social Responsibility

THE
SELF-ESTEEM
WORKBOOK

SECOND EDITION

GLENN R. SCHIRALDI, PhD

NEW HARBINGER PUBLICATIONS, INC.

Publisher's Note

This publication is designed to provide accurate and authoritative information in regard to the subject matter covered. It is sold with the understanding that the publisher is not engaged in rendering psychological, financial, legal, or other professional services. If expert assistance or counseling is needed, the services of a competent professional should be sought.

Distributed in Canada by Raincoast Books

Copyright © 2016 by Glenn R. Schiraldi
          New Harbinger Publications, Inc.
          5674 Shattuck Avenue
          Oakland, CA 94609
          www.newharbinger.com

Cover design by Amy Shoup

Acquired by Tesilya Hanauer

Edited by James Lainsbury

Library of Congress Cataloging-in-Publication Data on file

Printed in the United States of America

22   21   20

15   14   13   12   11   10

When we plant a rose seed in the earth, we notice that it is small, but we do not criticize it as "rootless and stemless." We treat it as a seed, giving it the water and nourishment required of a seed. When it first shoots up out of the earth, we don't condemn it as immature and underdeveloped, nor do we criticize the buds for not being open when they appear. We stand in wonder at the process taking place and give the plant the care it needs at each stage of its development. The rose is a rose from the time it is a seed to the time it dies. Within it, at all times, it contains its whole potential. It seems to be constantly in the process of change; yet at each state, at each moment, it is [whole] as it is (Gallwey 1974).

I dedicate this work to my angel mother, who—like so many mothers throughout history—quietly modeled so many of the principles described herein.

Contents

Preface to the Second Edition   xi
Introduction   1

Part I: Understanding Self-Esteem

1   Why Self-Esteem?   5
2   Getting Ready—The Physical Preparations   9
3   Self-Esteem and How It Develops   23

Part II: The Skills of Self-Esteem

Factor I: The Reality of Unconditional Human Worth

4   The Basics of Human Worth   33
5   Recognize and Replace Self-Defeating Thoughts   43
6   Acknowledge Reality—"Nevertheless!"   57
7   Regard Your Core Worth   61
8   Create the Habit of Core-Affirming Thoughts   67
9   An Overview of Unconditional Human Worth   71

Factor II: Experiencing Unconditional Love

10   The Basics of Unconditional Love   77
11   Find, Love, and Heal the Core Self   83
12   The Language of Love   89
13   The Appreciative Opinion of Others   95
14   Acknowledge and Accept Positive Qualities   97
15   Cultivate Body Appreciation   103
16   Reinforce and Strengthen Body Appreciation   109
17   Assert Self-Love and Appreciation   113
18   Eyes of Love Meditation   117
19   Liking the Face in the Mirror   119
20   See Yourself Through Loving Eyes   121
21   Experience Love at the Heart Level   125

22   Self-Compassion and Mindful Awareness   129
23   Meet Pain with Self-Compassion   137
24   Experience Self-Compassion at the Body Level   145
25   Compassionate Journaling   149
26   An Overview of Unconditional Love   157

Factor III: The Active Side of Love: Growing

27   The Basics of Growing   161
28   Accept That You Aren't Perfect   169
29   Just for the Fun of It (Contemplating Possibilities)   173
30   Take Stock of Your Character   177
31   Practice Forgiving   183
32   Experience Wholesome Pleasure   193
33   Prepare for Setbacks   203
34   An Overview of Growing   213

Epilogue: Summing Up   217

Acknowledgments   219

Appendices

Appendix I: Guidelines for Helping the Person in Distress   223
Appendix II: Forgiving the Self   227
Appendix III: Touching the Past with Love   231

Recommended Resources   235

Bibliography   239

Preface to the Second Edition

Since the first edition of *The Self-Esteem Workbook* appeared in 2001, it has been most gratifying to learn that it has helped so many people feel happier and more whole. Readers have said that they appreciate that the workbook is user-friendly, complete, and concise. Recent research, however, suggests that several important additions and revisions be included in this edition:

1. Chapter 2, "Getting Ready—The Physical Preparations," has been revised to reflect our new understanding of brain plasticity—and how sleep, exercise, and nutrition greatly influence brain function and mental health.

2. Research demonstrates that genuine, mature love changes us in significant and beneficial ways—physiologically and psychologically. Therefore, I added six important chapters to support the second building block of self-esteem, unconditional love:

   a. Chapter 20 uses art to experience love and elicit emotions in ways that language and logic do not.

   b. Chapter 21 teaches you how to increase heart coherence. The heart coherence skill will help you experience love at the heart level, which, in turn, profoundly affects mood. This is a powerful complement to cognitive strategies.

   c. Self-compassion is a powerful antidote to self-criticism and the usual ways we try to confront the inevitable pains of life. Four chapters (22, 23, 24, and 25) encourage us to bring kindness rather than harshness to our daily experiences, thus honoring and respecting who we are at the core.

3. Chapter 31, on forgiveness, encourages us to replace anger, which shuts down the heart, with love, so that we can move beyond the past, get back in touch with our loving nature, and be free to grow.

4. Stress is something we all face. Appendix I has been expanded to reflect what we've learned in recent years, tying together stress, trauma, grief, and self-esteem.

5. I also revised and expanded the "Recommended Resources" section to provide more useful aids to building self-esteem.

Despite these important changes, *The Self-Esteem Workbook* retains the reassuring theme that healthy, secure self-esteem is within the reach of everyone, no matter how difficult one's path has been.

Wholesome self-esteem is cultivated by practicing skills linked to the three building blocks of self-esteem: unconditional human worth, unconditional love, and growth. My sincere hope is that the skills in this workbook will provide uplift and support in your life's journey.

Note: Worksheet versions of many of the exercises in this book are available for download at http://www.newharbinger.com/35937. See the back of this book for more information.

Introduction

We need to see ourselves as basic miracles.

—Virginia Satir

Self-esteem is not the only determinant of happiness. Certainly it is one of the most important.

The beloved late comedian George Burns observed that most of the things that make people happy—health, marriage, raising a family, self-respect, and so forth—do not fall into our laps. We "have to work at them a little" (1984).

And so it is with self-esteem. Like cultivating a garden, building self-esteem involves consistent effort. The program described in this book takes approximately a half hour a day, more or less, over a 150-day period. Is this investment worth it? When we consider how great the effect of self-esteem is on mental and physical well-being, in both the short and long term, few efforts seem more worthwhile.

The program you are about to start is the central component of Stress and the Healthy Mind, a course that I developed and taught at the University of Maryland. The course has been found to raise self-esteem while reducing symptoms of depression, anxiety, and hostility among adults eighteen to sixty-eight years of age (Schiraldi and Brown 2001; Brown and Schiraldi 2000). Although intended for adults, the principles and skills in this book are equally applicable to adolescents and, when slightly simplified, children.

Part I

Understanding Self-Esteem

CHAPTER 1

Why Self-Esteem?

How fortunate is the person with self-esteem. There is general agreement that self-esteem is central to good mental and physical health, while self-dislike degrades health and performance. Self-dislike appears to contribute to:

- Depression

- Anxiety

- Stress and trauma symptoms

- Psychosomatic illness, like headaches, insomnia, fatigue, and digestive tract upset

- Hostility, excessive or deep-seated anger, dislike and distrust of others, and competitiveness

- Spouse and child abuse

- Entering into abusive or unhappy relationships

- Alcohol and drug abuse

- Eating disorders and unhealthy dieting

- Poor communication (for example, nonassertive, aggressive, defensive, critical, or sarcastic styles)

- Promiscuity

- Dependency

- Sensitivity to criticism

- Tendency to put on a false front to impress others

- Social difficulties, such as withdrawal and loneliness

- Poor performance

- Preoccupation with problems

- Status concern

- Criminality

It's no wonder self-dislike is called the "invisible handicap." Conversely, self-esteem is highly correlated to overall life satisfaction and happiness around the world. In a 1992 Gallup survey, 89 percent of respondents said that self-esteem is very important in motivating a person to work hard and succeed. Self-esteem was ranked higher as a motivator than any other variable. It is not surprising, therefore, that those with self-esteem are more likely to engage in healthy behaviors. Those with self-esteem tend to be friendlier, more expressive, more active, more self-trusting and trusting of others, and less troubled by inner problems and criticism (Coopersmith 1967). When mental disorders do strike, those with self-esteem tend to respond better to professional help, and recovering alcoholics with self-esteem are less likely to relapse (Mecca, Smelser, and Vasconcellos 1989). (See "Appendix I: Guidelines for Helping the Person in Distress" to better understand how stress, mental health, and self-esteem interrelate.) Indeed, one searches the literature in vain to find a disadvantage of having healthy, secure self-esteem. Thus, an assumption of this book is that self-esteem not only helps reduce undesired stress and illness symptoms, but also is an essential foundation for human growth.

Despite the importance of self-esteem, the psychotherapeutic community has focused surprisingly little attention on building it directly rather than indirectly. For example, an oft-stated aim of psychotherapy is to build self-esteem. However, the assumption that reducing illness symptoms will indirectly build self-esteem is generally unsupported. Lacking a comprehensive approach, some well-intending individuals have prescribed quick fixes based on unsound principles, which can actually damage self-esteem in the long run.

This book provides a step-by-step plan based on sound principles to help you build a healthy, realistic, and generally stable self-esteem. The approach requires that the skills herein be applied and practiced. Merely having knowledge is not enough. Each self-esteem skill is based on mastery of the skills that precede it. As Abraham Maslow noted, developing self-esteem requires many and major impacts (Lowry 1973). Therefore, resist the tendency to read through this book quickly. Instead, commit now to applying and mastering each skill before moving on to try the next one.

To Begin

The following checkup will provide you with a starting point from which to measure your progress with building self-esteem as you read through this book. Taking the checkup will also begin the process of reinforcing some of the goals of this book. It is comforting to realize that each person already possesses some measure of self-esteem to build on. There is nothing tricky about this checkup, nor is it important how your scores compare with the scores of others. So just relax and be as completely honest as you can.

The Self-Esteem Checkup

First, rate from 0 to 10 how much you believe each of the following statements: 0 means you completely disbelieve it, whereas 10 means you think it is completely true.

Statement	Rating
1. I am a worthwhile person.	7
2. I am as valuable a person as anyone else.	10
3. I have the qualities I need to live well.	5
4. When I look into my eyes in the mirror, I have a pleasant feeling.	4
5. I don't feel like an overall failure.	5
6. I can laugh at myself.	7
7. I am happy to be me.	6
8. I like myself, even when others reject me.	6
9. I love and support myself, regardless of what happens.	4
10. I am generally satisfied with the way I am developing as a person.	4
11. I respect myself.	4
12. I'd rather be me than someone else.	7
Total score	

Next, rate your self-esteem on the following scales (Gauthier, Pellerin, and Renaud 1983):

0   69   100

Total lack of self-esteem   Total fullness of self-esteem

Your response _____

How often do you feel restricted in your daily activities because of difficulties with self-esteem?

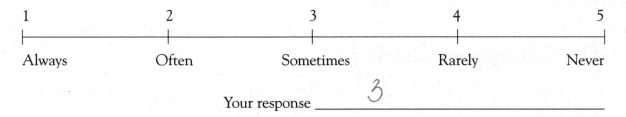

1	2	3	4	5
Always	Often	Sometimes	Rarely	Never

Your response _____3_____

How serious is your problem with self-esteem?

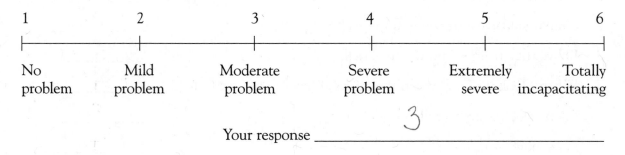

1	2	3	4	5	6
No problem	Mild problem	Moderate problem	Severe problem	Extremely severe	Totally incapacitating

Your response _____3_____

CHAPTER 2

Getting Ready—
The Physical Preparations

The mind and body are connected. If you want to feel your best mentally, take good care of your body, which includes your brain. This only stands to reason. So often people who feel stressed, fatigued, and mentally "down" are underexercised, undernourished, and underrested. Often, they assume that tending to the body takes too much time or is too difficult. So they hope for a quick fix that allows them to ignore their basic physical needs, while their mental health and performance suffer. The point is important enough to restate: you can't ignore your body and expect to feel good. Time invested in physical health is a wise investment indeed. It saves time by sharpening your performance. More importantly, it improves your mood. Your mood, in turn, will influence how you experience yourself.

The object of this chapter is to help you set up and execute a simple written plan for optimal physical health in three areas: regular exercise, sleep, and eating practices.

Brain Plasticity

Stress and aging tend to damage, shrink, or impair brain cells (neurons), particularly in areas of the brain responsible for thinking and regulating emotions. Fortunately, the harmful effects of stress and aging can be minimized and even reversed through healthy eating, exercise, and sleep. We have learned that what improves the health of the heart, and physical health generally, also improves brain health, mood, and brain function. The steps in this chapter work together to optimize the brain by

- increasing blood flow to the brain;

- flushing toxins from the brain;

- strengthening and regrowing neurons, the connections between neurons, and supportive tissues;

- decreasing inflammation and oxidative stress within neurons;

- strengthening the blood-brain barrier, which prevents toxins and molecules that cause inflammation from entering the brain; and

- promoting body leanness, which favors brain health.

Think of the brain as a computer. We might have powerful software, which is like the self-esteem strategies we'll explore later, but if the brain's hardware (the health and functioning of the neurons) is sluggish, the computer won't function optimally. So this chapter will help us strengthen brain hardware, while also improving physical health and mood generally.

Regular Exercise

Exercise improves self-esteem and mental health overall. It also improves sleep, increases energy, helps to regulate stress, and promotes leanness.

The goal is at least thirty minutes of aerobic exercise (rhythmic, continuous exercise, such as brisk walking, biking, swimming, stair climbing, and jogging) all or most days. Strength (resistance) training and flexibility training confer additional benefits. If time permits, add these to your program. If you can't, or if adding these appears overwhelming, then be content with aerobic exercise. Any amount of exercise is better than none. Even a ten-minute "energy walk," a break from sitting at the desk, has been found to increase energy and lift the mood (Thayer 1989).

Start exercising gently, and build up very gradually. You are not in a competition with anyone. Exercise should leave you feeling refreshed and energized. It should not hurt or exhaust you beyond a pleasant fatigue. If you can eventually work up to thirty minutes or more of aerobic exercise on most days, great. If not, do what you can to start. Do make a plan for regular exercise. If you have trouble falling asleep, try exercising before dinner, or earlier. Early morning exercise helps to regulate sleep rhythms. Exercising in the sunlight also helps the body produce vitamin D, which improves brain function in many ways. Consult your physician if you are over forty years old, if you have any known risk factors for cardiovascular disease, or if you have any concerns about starting an exercise program.

Sleep Hygiene

Many studies (Diener 1984) have associated poor sleep with unhappiness. Fortunately, researchers in recent years have identified many ways to improve sleep. Three considerations for sleep are crucial: amount, regularity, and quality.

An appropriate amount of sleep. Most adults require at least seven and a half hours of sleep each night. Adults who average near that amount, but then get an additional hour to an hour and a half of sleep per night, typically feel better and perform better. However, today's lifestyle nibbles away at our sleep time to the point that many adults are chronically sleep deprived. As little as twenty to thirty minutes of additional sleep a night can significantly improve mood and performance. Many sleep researchers recommend that most people get at least eight hours of sleep per night.

Regularity of sleep. Regular sleep and wake-up times are needed to keep the body's sleep cycle consistent. Retiring at irregular hours (for example, getting to bed much later on Friday and Saturday nights than on the weekdays) can lead to exhaustion and insomnia.

So, the idea behind good sleep hygiene is to get a little more sleep than you think you need and to keep sleep and wake-up times as consistent as possible throughout the week, varying no more than one hour from night to night—even on weekends.

Sleep quality. Make the bedroom a peaceful place for sleeping. Keep phones, computers, televisions, bills, work, and arousing reading out of the bedroom. Turn off lights and light-emitting electronic devices at least an hour before retiring (the blue light from electronic devices is particularly disruptive to sleep). Make sure that early morning sunlight does not enter through windows. Eliminate noise or obscure it with white noise (for example, a fan or nature sounds). Avoid having meals within four hours of retiring. Reduce or avoid stimulants like caffeine and nicotine for at least seven hours before bedtime. Alcohol hastens sleep, but it later acts as a stimulant that fragments sleep, so avoid alcohol in the hours before bedtime. Talk to your doctor if snoring or sleep apnea is preventing a good night's sleep.

Eating Practices

Numerous studies indicate that Mediterranean-style eating practices, as captured by the US Department of Health and Human Services' *2015–2020 Dietary Guidelines for Americans*, benefit the brain. Such practices are rich in brain-protecting antioxidants, minerals, and vitamins. These eating practices are

- high in fish and plant foods (vegetables, fruits, seeds, nuts, whole grains, herbs, beans, peas, lentils, olive or canola oil) and

- low in animal (or saturated) fats (for example, red and processed meats, high-fat dairy products), refined grains, sugar-sweetened food and drinks, and processed and fast foods (which typically contain sugar, salt, refined flour, preservatives, and unhealthy fats—all of which are to be minimized).

Brain-friendly eating practices follow these guidelines:

- Consume most of your calories from plant foods. Fresh, frozen, and minimally processed plant foods are usually best, since they tend to have less added sugar, salt, and fat and contain more fiber.

- Minimize meat, especially red and processed meats (for example, corned beef, bacon, ham, salami, hot dogs). Reduce the size of meat servings and choose, whenever possible, lean meats, such as poultry without the skin. Instead of meat, each week have several servings of seafood or meat alternatives, such as beans, peas, lentils, nuts, or seeds. Think of your plate filled mostly with plant foods, with meat as a side dish, and you'll get a good idea of these first two guidelines.

- Keep blood sugar steady throughout the day by eating a good breakfast and not skipping meals. Have a high-quality protein source (for example, eggs or yogurt) at breakfast and distribute protein equally among meals. Concentrated sweets cause blood sugar to fluctuate, so minimize sugar-sweetened sodas, cookies, and the like.

- Stay hydrated. Drink plenty of liquids throughout the day, because even slight dehydration can impair mood and functioning. Depending on weight, activity, and ambient conditions, you might need up to thirteen cups of liquid or more to maintain optimal brain function and mood. Check the water at the bottom of the toilet bowl after urinating; urine that is clear or pale yellow indicates adequate fluid intake. Drinking two glasses of water before meals has also been found to promote weight loss.

- Avoid excesses of any drug. Brain imaging shows that any drug in excess, including caffeine, alcohol, nicotine, and so-called recreational drugs, can adversely affect brain function years before structural changes are apparent. These substances can also impair sleep.

Take Care of Your Body: A Written Plan

There is power in making a written plan and committing to stick to it. Please make a plan that you can follow, and begin to practice it for the next fourteen days. You'll actually stay with this plan throughout the entire course of this book and beyond, so make a realistic plan that you can comfortably keep. It is perfectly alright to give yourself several days to "work up" to the goals in your plan.

1. **Exercise** thirty to ninety minutes all or most days of the week, striving for at least thirty minutes of aerobic exercise daily. Describe your plan below:

2. **Sleep** _____ hours (a little more than you think you need) each night from _____ (time you'll retire) to _____ (time you'll wake up)

3. **Eat** at least three times a day, using healthy choices. Make a written week's menu using the "Sample Menu: A Week of Meals" worksheet, and check it against the guidelines that follow.

Dietary Guidelines

These dietary guidelines, which are appropriate for most people nineteen years and older, will help ensure that your sample weekly menu provides the nutrients you need to feel and function at your best. After reviewing them, make a sample weekly menu. Then check to see how well your sample menu meets the guidelines.

1. Does your plan provide the needed servings from each food group, as indicated below? (Someone trying to control weight would use the smaller figure for servings.)

Food Group	How Much Is Needed Each Day	What Counts As...	Comments/Provides
Fruits	1½–2 cups	**1 cup** In general, 1 cup of fruit or 100% fruit juice 1 large banana/orange/peach, 1 medium pear, or 1 small apple ½ cup dried fruit	Fruits and vegetables provide fiber and energy and many vitamins, minerals, and phytochemicals that reduce risk of various diseases (for example, potassium lowers the risk of high blood pressure).
Vegetables	2–3 cups	**1 cup** In general, 1 cup of raw or cooked vegetables or vegetable juice, or 2 cups of raw, leafy greens 1 cup of dry beans and peas (black, garbanzo, soybean/tofu, split peas, lentils, and so forth). Count these here or in the protein group, but not both.	Seek a variety of colorful fruits and vegetables—green, red, orange, yellow, and white. Several times a week include cruciferous vegetables, such as broccoli, cauliflower, cabbage, brussels sprouts, and kale.

Grains	5–8 ounce-equivalents	**1 ounce-equivalent** 1 slice bread or minibagel 1 cup ready-to-eat cereal (check label) ½ cup cooked rice, pasta, or cereal 3 cups popped popcorn 1 pancake (4½ inches) or 1 small tortilla (6 inches) ½ English muffin	Most servings should be *whole grains*, which reduce the risk of heart and other diseases. Whole grains contain fiber, B vitamins, antioxidants, minerals, and various plant chemicals. Whole grains include oatmeal, whole wheat, bulgur, whole barley, popcorn, and brown or wild rice.
Protein	5–6½ ounce-equivalents	**1 ounce-equivalent** 1 ounce of cooked fish, poultry, or lean meat 1 egg ¼ cup cooked dry beans and peas 1 tablespoon peanut butter ½ ounce of nuts or seeds	Most or all days should include nuts, seeds, and/or cooked dry beans and peas (for example, pinto beans, kidney beans, lentils, soybeans/tofu, or other soybean products). Note that ½ ounce of nuts equals 12 almonds, 24 pistachios, or 7 walnut halves. The fats in fish are particularly beneficial for the brain. Aim for at least 2 to 3 servings of fish per week, totaling at least 8 ounces.
Dairy	3 cups	**1 cup** 1 cup of low-fat or fat-free milk, yogurt, or calcium-fortified soymilk 1½ ounces of low-fat or fat-free natural cheese, such as Swiss or cheddar 2 ounces of low-fat or fat-free processed cheese (American)	Dairy is a major source of calcium, potassium, protein, B vitamins, and other vitamins and minerals.

Food Group	How Much Is Needed Each Day	What Counts As...	Comments/Provides
Oils	5–7 teaspoon-equivalents (an allowance, not a food group)	**1 teaspoon-equivalent** 1 teaspoon vegetable oil 1 teaspoon soft margarine 1 teaspoon mayonnaise 1 tablespoon salad dressing ½ tablespoon peanut butter	Oils provide needed unsaturated fatty acids and vitamin E. Olive and canola oils are particularly beneficial. Avoid trans and hydrogenated fats found in commercially made snacks, baked goods, stick margarine, and fried fast foods.
Empty Calories (mostly saturated fats and/or added sugars)	Not needed or recommended. Try to limit to 10% or less of your total caloric intake. Many prefer to "spend" these calories on other food groups.	**Calories in typical serving sizes:** 12 ounces of a sweetened soft drink or fruit punch = 150 calories 1 slice of cheesecake (⅛ of ½ a 9-inch cake) = 620 calories 1 tablespoon of jelly or jam = 50 calories 12 ounces of light beer = 110 calories 2-ounce candy bar = 250 calories 1 cup of ice cream = 400 calories 1 ounce of corn chips = 152 calories 1 jelly donut = 290 calories	

* Adapted from *2015–2020 Dietary Guidelines for Americans*. See www.ChooseMyPlate.gov for more detailed guidelines and a wealth of practical information about nutrition and physical activity. Except for dairy, amounts above depend on age, sex, and level of physical activity. The amounts needed assume you expend 1,600 to 2,400 calories per day. Males who are younger or more active, for example, might need to consume amounts at the higher range, or sometimes more.

2. Does your plan provide variety in order to get all needed nutrients? That is, do you vary your choices within each group? (For example, instead of an apple each day, try bananas or berries as alternatives.)

3. Does your plan follow the other guidelines discussed earlier in the "Eating Practices" section? (Note: If you prefer to plan online and see how well your dietary and physical activity choices compare to recommended amounts, go to http://www.ChooseMyPlate.gov and locate the federal government's excellent free tool, SuperTracker.)

CHAPTER 3

Self-Esteem and How It Develops

What leads to self-esteem? The research is very clear. If you want to have self-esteem, it helps to choose your parents well. Children with self-esteem tend to have parents who model self-esteem. These parents consistently are loving toward their children, expressing interest in the child's life and friends, giving time and encouragement. I am reminded of the man who said to his neighbor, "Why did you spend all day with your son fixing that bike when the bike shop could have fixed it in an hour?" The neighbor replied, "Because I am building a son, not fixing a bike."

Parents of children with self-esteem have high standards and expectations, but the expectations are clear, reasonable, consistent, and given with support and encouragement. The disciplinary style is democratic, which is to say that the child's opinions and individuality are respected, but the parents make the final decisions on matters of importance.

In effect, the parents give messages that say, "I trust you, but I also recognize that you are not perfect. Still, I love you, and therefore I will take time to guide you, set limits, discipline you, and expect the best of you because I believe in you and value you." These messages are far different from the distrust conveyed by the authoritarian parent or the lack of caring conveyed by the permissive parent.

Some individuals have none of these parental antecedents, yet still they have self-esteem. So this leads to a most important question: In the absence of these antecedents, how does one build self-esteem? Most assume we get value from what we do; from skills, character traits, and talents; or from the acceptance of others. Again, I suggest that none of these make a good starting place for self-esteem building. Where, then, do we start? Let's begin by examining what self-esteem is.

What Is Self-Esteem?

In principle, self-esteem is generally stable, but it can fluctuate, even from day to day, according to thought patterns, which can be influenced by, among other things, physical health, chemistry, appearance, and relationships. The fact that self-esteem can fluctuate is reason for optimism, because it suggests that self-esteem can change.

The definition of self-esteem is central to our journey. "Self-esteem" is a realistic, appreciative opinion of oneself. "Realistic" means accurate and honest. "Appreciative" implies positive feelings and liking oneself. Some speak of high and low self-esteem, but this makes self-esteem seem like a numbers game that is competitive and comparative. It's preferable to simply say that people possess self-esteem when they have a realistic and appreciative opinion of themselves. The figure below clarifies the meaning of self-esteem. Self-esteem is squarely between "self-defeating shame" and "self-defeating pride."

Self-defeating shame   Self-esteem   Self-defeating pride

People with *self-defeating pride* are trying to be more than human. They are arrogant and narcissistic, which means they think they are better and more important than others as a person. Their view of others is vertical, or comparative, which is to say that to be on top means others must be below them. Self-defeating pride is often rooted in insecurity. If you explore the lives of famous dictators, you often find a complete lack of the parental antecedents that I discussed earlier.

People with *self-defeating shame*, or *self-defeating humility*, believe that they are less than human. They view people vertically, and they see themselves as the dust of the earth. They hold an unrealistic and unappreciative opinion of themselves.

In contrast to the views above, people with *self-esteem* believe they are neither more nor less than human. Knowing their faults and rough edges, they still are deeply and quietly glad to be who they are (Briggs 1977). They are like the good friends who know you well and like you anyway because they recognize the goodness, excellence, and potential that coexist alongside imperfections. People with self-esteem view others as equals, on a level or horizontal plane.

Concepts Related to Self-Esteem

Self-esteem is often ignored because it and its related concepts can be somewhat confusing and complex. Let's disentangle some of this confusion by clarifying concepts that are related to self-esteem.

Identity

"Identity" answers these questions: Who am I? What defines me and my essential character? Identity provides a sense of oneself and one's individuality (for example, a woman's identity derived only from her role as a wife; a paraplegic's identity defined not by a crippled body, but by the real or inner self).

Appreciate

To appreciate is to think well of, to value, and to enjoy; to recognize gratefully; and to *rightly* estimate the quality or worth of someone or something.

Accept

To accept is to receive (that is, to take in as one's own) favorably and with pleasure, to approve, to believe in, and to respond favorably to someone or something. *Self-acceptance* is believing in oneself and receiving oneself favorably and with pleasure. One may accurately acknowledge one's weaknesses, be determined to improve, and still accept oneself. The internal dialogue might be something like this: *I acknowledge my faults. I love myself, though not necessarily all of my behaviors. As I improve my behavior, I can feel good about me and my behavior.*

Self-Confidence

"Self-confidence" usually refers to a belief in one's abilities; it's related to competence and self-efficacy. As one's competence increases, one's confidence increases. In the broader and deeper sense, *self-confidence* is a belief in oneself as a person, leading to a general sense of "I can do it." Self-confident people might say to themselves, *Because anyone can do just about anything—given enough time, practice, experience, resources, and so forth—why can't I? I may not succeed completely or quickly, but the direction will be desirable.* Demonstrating competence is satisfying, but it is an outgrowth of self-worth, not a way to establish it.

Competence and confidence correlate with self-esteem but are not causal. If we base feelings of worth on competence and achievements, then if we fail there is no worth.

Pride

English minister Charles Caleb Colton (1780–1832) wrote that pride "makes some men ridiculous, but prevents others from becoming so." As this quote alludes to, there are two sides to pride as it relates to self-esteem: self-defeating and healthy.

As discussed previously, "self-defeating pride" is the attitude that one is superior, more valuable, or more important as a person than others. Such people also perceive themselves as more capable, self-sufficient, or infallible than they actually are. Synonyms for self-defeating pride include "haughtiness," "arrogance," "conceit," "pretentiousness" (that is, trying to impress), "vanity" (that is, excessive desire or need to be admired), and "narcissism" (that is, selfishness, a grandiose sense of self, an exploitive nature). Self-defeating pride is typically rooted in fear (as in fear of being vulnerable) and/or the need to defend oneself.

"Healthy pride" is a realistic sense of one's own dignity or worth; self-respect; and gratitude and delight in one's achievements, talents, service, or membership (that is, in family, race, and so forth).

Humility

There also are two sides to humility: self-defeating humility and healthy humility. "Self-defeating humility" is spineless submissiveness, contemptibility, and an abject lack of self-respect (that is, "dust of the earth").

"Healthy humility," on the other hand, involves the absence of self-defeating pride, the recognition of one's imperfections or weaknesses, a consciousness of one's own shortcomings and ignorance, and teachableness. It is the realization that all are of equal worth. Healthy humility relates to meek behavior (in the positive sense), meaning one is mild, patient, and not easily stirred to anger.

Healthy humility and healthy pride coexist in a person with self-esteem: humility because one realizes how much one still has to learn, and pride in recognizing the dignity and worth one shares with all other humans.

The following amusing story (De Mello 1990) relates to one lacking in healthy humility:

A guru advised a scholar: "Go out in the rain and raise your arms upward. That'll bring you a revelation."

The next day the scholar reported back. "When I followed your advice, water flowed down my neck," he told the guru. "I felt like a complete fool."

"For the first day, that's quite a revelation," replied the guru.

Selfishness

Some mistakenly equate selfishness with self-esteem. So let's state an important principle: the purpose of self-esteem is to transcend the self. Self-consciousness is a painful situation that keeps one's focus inward. Healing the pain with love enables one's focus to expand outward, making one freer to love others and enjoy life. The person with self-esteem loves by choice from a secure base (as opposed, say, to a codependent individual who possesses neither self-esteem nor choice). Thus, building self-esteem warrants our best efforts.

Cost-Benefit Analysis

Some people do not build self-esteem because they don't know how. But others resist building self-esteem, as difficult as that may be to believe, because there are apparent advantages to self-dislike. Before investing the time to build self-esteem, let's do what an effective manager would do before considering a new plan: a cost-benefit analysis. First, list all of the advantages of self-dislike you can think of. When you are finished, list all of the disadvantages.

Examples of Advantages for Self-Dislike

- No risk. I have no expectations of myself, nor do others. I can be lazy and set low goals. I'll rarely disappoint myself or others.

- The world is predictable. I understand when people don't accept me because I don't accept myself. I understand not having to try.

- Sometimes I get pity and attention, at least initially.

- It is a family norm. When I follow the pattern, I feel like I fit in.

- It keeps me from developing self-defeating pride.

- It justifies my poor dressing and grooming habits.

Examples of Disadvantages of Self-Dislike

- It is very painful.

- Life is no fun.

- It leads to psychosomatic symptoms and disease.

- It creates a vicious cycle: Because I have a low opinion of myself, I don't try. Then others treat me poorly. They interpret my pessimism and apathy as indicators of incompetence. Their poor treatment of me confirms my low opinion of myself.

Your Personal Advantages and Disadvantages

Pros/Advantages
(The good thing about self-dislike is…)

Cons/Disadvantages
(The bad thing about self-dislike is…)

Benefits of Emotional Change

This analysis raises some very important questions. The ultimate question, of course, is this: Is self-dislike a problem for me in terms of emotional, physical, or social costs? Other questions include: Are there ways to build self-esteem and still get my desires for attention, help, security, and so forth met? Am I willing to risk losing some of the payoffs of self-dislike in order to get the gains of self-esteem?

Some find it helpful to test the waters before beginning to change. Try answering this question: What would be the positive consequences of having a realistic and appreciative opinion of myself?

What follows are some sample responses:

- I'd be less susceptible to persuasion.

- I'd be less driven by fear.

- I'd be more motivated by enjoyment and personal satisfaction.

- I'd be happier.

- I'd try more.

- I'd risk more.

- I'd be more at ease with my rough edges and more willing to work on them.

- I'd be happier with my relationships and less likely to stick with partners who aren't worth it.

- I'd be more comfortable with expressing my feelings.

- I'd be less selfish and self-protective.

- I'd question myself and my actions less when things go wrong.

- I'd worry less.

- I'd be more likely to be respected and treated well.

- I'd be considered more attractive.

- I'd enjoy life more.

- I'd make better, more objective decisions.

- I'd feel liked for who I am, and not for some phony person I wish I were.

Write your answers below.

How to Build Self-Esteem

To change self-esteem is to first understand the factors on which it is built. Self-esteem is based on three sequential factors: (1) unconditional human worth, (2) love, and (3) growing.

The Foundations of Self-Esteem

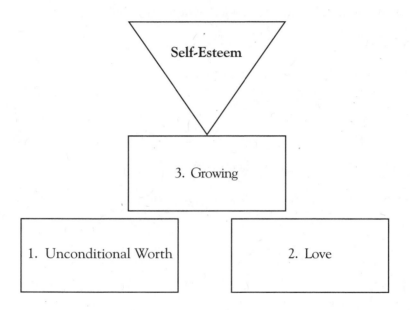

While all three factors are essential to building self-esteem, the *sequence* is crucial. Self-esteem is based first on unconditional worth, then love, and then growing. "Growing" (or "coming to flower") refers to moving in the desired direction. Many people become frustrated when trying to build self-esteem because they start with growth and neglect the first two important factors: unconditional worth and love. Without a secure base, self-esteem topples. So a methodical approach that avoids shortcuts is best.

The remainder of this book sequentially deals with building the skills necessary to master each of the essential factors for building healthy self-esteem: the section called "Factor I" focuses on unconditional human worth; the section called "Factor II" addresses love; and the section called "Factor III" focuses on growing.

PART II

THE SKILLS OF SELF-ESTEEM

The Reality of Unconditional Human Worth

CHAPTER 4

The Basics of Human Worth

"Unconditional human worth" means that you are important and valuable as a person because your essential, core self is unique and precious; of infinite, eternal, unchanging value; and good. Unconditional human worth implies that you are as precious as any other person.

Howard's Laws of Human Worth

Unconditional human worth is beautifully described by five axioms, which I call Howard's Laws, based on the work of Claudia A. Howard (1992).

1. All have infinite, internal, eternal, and unconditional worth *as people*.

2. All have equal worth as people. Worth is not comparative or competitive. Although you might be better at sports, academics, or business, and I might be better with social skills, we both have equal worth as human beings.

3. Externals neither add to nor diminish worth. Externals include things like money, looks, performance, and achievements. These only increase one's *market* or *social* worth. Worth as a person, however, is infinite and unchanging.

4. Worth is stable and never in jeopardy (even if someone rejects you).

5. Worth doesn't have to be earned or proved. It already exists. Just recognize, accept, and appreciate it.

The Core Self

The "human core," sometimes called the essential, spiritual self, is like the spherical crystal with facets that beautifully reflect sunlight.

The Core Self

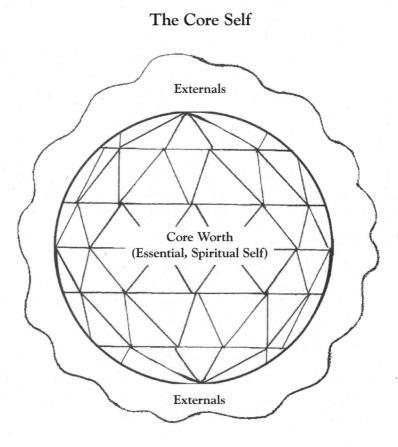

Much like a newborn baby, the core is fundamentally right and whole—complete, but not completed. "*Completed*" means fully developed and finished. A person is *complete* in the sense that each of us has every attribute, in embryo, that everyone else has—every attribute that is needed. The core is beautiful, lovable, and full of potential. This anecdote, told by George Durrant (1980), himself a kind and loving teacher, demonstrates the inner quality of the core self:

> One man was wrestling on the floor with his children and he decided he was tired so he faked like he was dead. That's one way you can get a rest. And the little boys were very concerned and one was a little older than the other and pried open his daddy's eye and he said to his little brother with some reassurance, "He's still *in* there."

What's *in* there is the core self. Over time, the core becomes surrounded with externals. Like a dirty film on the surface of a body of water, some externals can hide the core. Other externals, like a halo, can brighten the core and allow its light to be seen or experienced. For example, mistakes or criticism may camouflage the core, making it difficult for one to see and experience one's worth. The love of others helps us feel our worth. A talent shared is one way to express worth. These change the way worth is experienced, not the worth itself.

Some people spend their lives trying to look good on the outside in order to cover up shame, or a feeling of worthlessness, on the inside. If, however, we use externals to fill the empty feeling at the core, we will remain unfulfilled, perhaps always seeking approval or becoming cynical. For example, psychiatrists tell us that their offices are filled with people who ask, "Doctor, I am successful. Why am I unhappy?"

It is impossible to earn core worth through personal performance or any other external. It already exists. Consider the following list of externals.

Worth As a Person Is Independent of Externals

Energy level	Material advantages	Church activity
Appearance or looks	Wealth	Worthiness
Strength	Mistakes	Blessings
Intelligence	Behavior	Family image
Education	Decisions	Parents' status or character
Gender	Position and status	Personality traits
Race, ethnicity, or skin color	Physical fitness	Marriage status
Scholastic achievement or grades	Manners	People you date
Skills	Net value or market worth	Power
Friendliness	Voice	Being right
Talents	Clothes	State of the economy or stock market
Creative ability	Car	Inexperience
Handicaps	Spirituality	

Present Functioning Level

Attitudes

Daily self-evaluations

Performance

Hygiene or grooming

Sickness or health

Productivity

Resilience

Confidence

Control over events

Selfishness or selflessness

Feelings

Comparisons

Competence relative to others (for example, in sports, in salary)

Judgments of Others

How many people like you

Approval or acceptance of others

How others treat you

Illustrative Examples

The person with self-esteem beholds and appreciates the core self. This person sees flaws as external to the core; they require attention, developing, nurturing, and acceptance when change is not possible. The following four examples illustrate the idea of core worth.

I take courage from a spirited young boy's example. Confined to a wheelchair, he matter-of-factly explained, "A tumor broke the nerve that tells my legs what to do." He knew how to separate worth from externals.

Another who radiates a quiet inner gladness is Ken Kirk, a former student of mine, who wrote this poem:

If I Could Be

If I could be a tree I would
provide shade for all mankind.

If I could be the sea I would
be calm for all to travel.

*If I could be the sun I would
provide warmth for all living things.*

*If I could be the wind I would
be a cool breeze on a hot summer day.*

*If I could be the rain I would
keep the earth fertile.*

*But, to be any one of these things would be to miss out on all the rest. And this is why,
if I could be anything I would be nothing more than me.*

The state of Virginia has several beautiful colonial bed-and-breakfast inns. Staying in one
with a lovely stone fireplace, I beheld an antique wooden duck. Large, plain, and unpainted,
perhaps carved by a colonial farmer, it added a simple touch of class to the homey room. Near
the fireplace was a large log, which I appreciated because the night was chilly. I asked my students which one had more worth, the wooden duck or the wooden log? One woman thoughtfully answered, "Their worth is the same. They are just different."

A schoolteacher friend of mine was in a bus with her students. The bus was struck by
another bus, resulting in a number of injuries. "After the accident," she reflected, "I watched
the children running around, assuming leadership and caring for each other, and then I could
truly see their worth." Events can help us to *see* worth, but they neither add to nor diminish
core worth.

Separating Worth from Externals

To separate core worth from externals is a primary goal of building self-esteem.

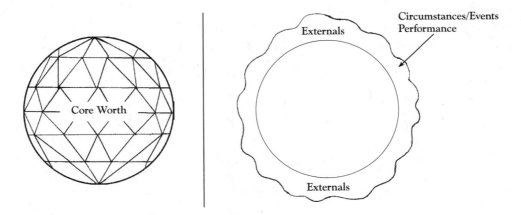

Used with the permission of Claudia A. Howard, Individual Potential Seminars, as are the next two diagrams.

The goal of separating worth from externals can be difficult in today's culture. Television programming and other entertainment media can convey the message that you are not worthwhile if you are not young, bold, beautiful, or wealthy. Fast-lane living in today's cities conveys the message that you must be high powered and successful to be somebody. Taken to the unrestrained extreme, today's work ethic suggests that one loses worth if one is sleeping, vacationing, or not producing.

Let's consider two ways to look at human worth: proposition one (the first figure) suggests that worth equals externals; proposition two (the second figure) suggests that worth is separate from externals.

When Worth Equals Externals

When worth equals externals, self-esteem rises and falls with events. For instance, a high school student may feel less worthwhile when she looks in the mirror and notices her complexion. But then she feels better when a cute guy says hello; when he fails to ask her for a date, she feels depressed. After a compliment on her dress, she feels great; after a tough math exam, she feels bad. She feels great when she and that guy begin dating, but she's miserable when they break up. She is on an emotional roller coaster.

For adults, the highs may come with promotions, awards, or graduation from medical school. The lows may come with criticism, poor performance, or a favored team losing a game.

If your worth equals your job or your marriage, how will you feel if you realize you have already received your last promotion or if you divorce? Your feelings will probably go beyond the normal and appropriate sadness and disappointment. When worth is in doubt, depression usually follows. If human worth equals market worth, then only the rich and powerful have worth. By this line of reasoning, a billionaire, or Hitler, would have more human worth than a Mother Teresa.

When Worth is Separate from Externals

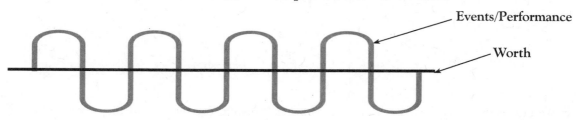

When worth is separate from externals, human worth is intrinsic and unchanging, irrespective of outside events or circumstances. Here, we distinguish feeling bad about events or behaviors (guilt) from feeling bad about the core self (shame). Guilt for foolish behavior is a healthy motivation for change. Condemning the core, however, saps motivation.

The idea is to judge behavior, but not the core. One can be reasonably objective in judging behaviors and present skill levels. It is difficult to be reasonable or objective when one has condemned the self at the core.

It is also wise to separate uncomfortable feelings arising from disappointment, illness, fatigue, chemical fluctuations, anger, anxiety, and the like from feeling bad about the core self.

Let's look at an example of a difficult situation. Let's say that someone else was awarded a promotion you desired. You tell yourself, "Perhaps some of my skills are not up to par yet for this job." This is a statement of fact that judges your skill level, experience, or training. And it would result in appropriate disappointment and perhaps the decision to improve your skills. On the other hand, if you tell yourself, "I'm not good enough as a person," this is a statement of worth that means you are inferior as a person. Obviously, this self-destructive choice in thinking would lead to self-dislike and perhaps depression. So judge your present skills and performance, never the core.

Why Individuals Have Worth

I dedicate this section to people who struggle with the notion of unconditional worth. I think of an accomplished fifty-year-old man who was attending a self-esteem class. Intellectual and bright, he listened to the axioms of human worth. He was struggling, looking like he wanted to believe them but unable to grasp why all human beings could have worth despite their imperfections and foolish behaviors. The light went on eventually, to his great pleasure.

I'd like to start by posing some questions: Why do people spend millions of dollars to extricate from a well a two-year-old girl who has never done anything of note? Why do we love a baby? How are we like a dog or an inanimate object? How are we different?

A human has worth for at least four reasons.

1. *Present endowments.* A human's innate nature is enjoyable. It is fun to watch a child play in the leaves or respond to the beauty of nature. It is fun to love children and see them respond with a smile, joy, a sense of play, affection, or the sense of security to take on the world with enthusiasm.

2. *Capacities.* When people behave obnoxiously, it is fun to ponder their potential to beautify life with art, craftsmanship, or other creations; with emotions of pleasure, acceptance, and encouragement; and with laughter, work, and love. Capacities are innate, and people are able to discover and develop them. When we err, we have the capacity to correct our course. Thus, we observe that human beings are fallible, but

infinitely perfectible, and have an "ability to convert not just their food, but also their hopes, into vital energy" (Cousins 1983). When theologians point to the notion that humans are created in God's image and likeness, they refer to the concept that a person is like a seed: whole. Like a seed, each person is complete but not completed, possessing in embryo every conceivable capacity: to think rationally, to emote, to sacrifice, to love, to make ethical choices, to recognize truth and worth, to create, to beautify, to be gentle, to be patient, and to be firm.

3. *Past contributions.* If one ever contributed to the well-being of others or self—in any way, large or small—then that person is not worthless.

4. *The craftsmanship of the body.* Although it is an external, the body is a nice metaphor for the core self. A number of influences in today's culture tend to "thing-ify" the body. The media glorifies using others as pleasure objects. Many individuals have been sexually or physically abused. When a body is mistreated, a person can come to see the body as disgusting. The greater danger is that the person will come to devalue the core self. On the other hand, considering the marvelous intricacies of the body with respect can help a person appreciate the worth of the core self. (We shall return to this important concept in chapters 15 and 16.)

Sometimes people ask, "What if I am ugly or disabled? How can I feel worthwhile?" I challenge them to pretend they are partially or completely paralyzed and to come up with ways they could still assert and experience their worth. The responses are often illuminating.

- I could convey love through my eyes.

- I could learn to allow people to help me and to enjoy their service.

- I could change my thoughts; I could learn to define myself as more than my body.

- I could demonstrate my will (for example, by appreciating what I see, by trying to move even a finger, by improving my mind).

We repeatedly return to the underlying concepts. Worth is already there. It is there whether you are sleeping or producing. The core is more than behavior, position, or any other external. Our challenge is to experience and enjoy that core worth.

Worth is neither comparative nor competitive, as is demonstrated by the experience of this father (Durrant 1980):

Three of my children were swinging at a park and two of them had learned to pump themselves in the swing and that's always a happy day for a father when his children learn to pump themselves in a swing. And two of them were going real high and Devon says, "I'm keeping up with Katherine," and Katherine looked across and said,

"I'm keeping up with Devon" 'cause they were swinging right together. And little Marinda was in the middle and she was just barely moving because there was a breeze. And little Marinda, hearing them saying they're keeping up with each other...said, "I'm just keeping up with myself."

Even at a young age, a child can understand the concept of intrinsic worth that is not comparative or competitive, and he or she will be better off for it.

Reflections on Unconditional and Equal Human Worth

Please ponder the reflections on human worth below. When you finish you'll be ready to begin the human worth skill-building activities, which are found in chapters 5 through 9.

We [are] equal inhabitants of a paradise of individuals in which everybody has the right to be understood.

—Richard Rorty

We hold these truths to be self-evident, that all men are created equal, that they are endowed by their Creator with certain unalienable Rights, that among those are Life, Liberty, and the pursuit of Happiness.

—Declaration of Independence

We are all basically the same human beings, who seek happiness and try to avoid suffering.

Everybody is my peer group.

Your feeling, "I am of no value," is wrong. Absolutely wrong.

—Dalai Lama

You're as good as anybody else.

—Spoken to Martin Luther King by his father

You're as good as anyone, but you're no better than anyone, and don't forget it.

—Spoken to legendary coach John Wooden by his father

All men are alike when asleep.

—Aristotle

[We] are made in the image of God—a good God, a God of beauty… God declared his creation good.

—Rebecca Manley Pippert

We need to see ourselves as basic miracles.

—Virginia Satir

Men can be human, with human frailties, and still be great.

—Stephen L. Richards

Heroes don't need lettermen jackets. We know who we are.

—Evel Knievel

Letting circumstances or others determine worth gives them inappropriate control and power.

—Anonymous

When our value as human beings depends on what we make with our hands and minds, we become victims of the fear tactics of our world. When productivity is our main way of overcoming self-doubt, we are extremely vulnerable to rejection and criticism and prone to inner anxiety and depression.

—Henri J. M. Nouwen

Every cliché you've ever heard about babies is true, it seems to me. They are soft and warm, fascinating, cute, and lovable. I never met one that wasn't, and it's a good thing too, because if babies weren't so cute and lovable maybe we wouldn't so gladly put up with the fact that they're so demanding and so much trouble.

Babies are pure potential. You pick up a little baby and you're amazed by how light it is, but you feel also that you're holding the future, the earth and the sky, the sun and the moon, and all of it, everything, is brand new.

Babies help us to put the changing world into perspective too. Changing the world has to wait, when it's time to change the baby.

—Charles Osgood

Chapter 5

Recognize and Replace Self-Defeating Thoughts

Although all humans are infinitely worthwhile, all do not necessarily have a sense of their own worth. One reason is that negative, depressing thought patterns can erode one's sense of worth. Please note that we're not saying that worth is eroded, only one's ability to experience it.

Consider this situation. The boss scowls as he passes John and Bill in the hall. John begins to feel down on himself as he thinks, *Oh, no! He's upset with me.* Bill only gets concerned, not disturbed, as he tells himself, *The boss is probably having another battle with the front office.* What is the difference between the two? Not the event, but the way John and Bill thought about the event.

A branch of psychology called *cognitive therapy* has identified specific thought patterns that attack self-esteem and lead to depression. These thought patterns have been learned. They can be unlearned. Cognitive therapy provides an effective, straightforward way to eliminate these self-destructive thoughts and replace them with more reasonable thoughts. The model, developed by psychologist Albert Ellis, is simple:

A ⟶ B ⟶ C

A stands for the *activating* (or upsetting) event. B is the *belief* (or automatic thoughts) that we tell ourselves about A. C is the emotional *consequences* (or feelings, such as worthlessness or depression). Most people think A causes C. In reality, it is B, our self-talk, that has the greater influence.

Automatic Thoughts and Distortions

Whenever an upsetting event occurs, automatic thoughts, or ATs, run through our mind. Although we're each capable of thinking reasonably about upsetting events, sometimes our automatic thoughts are distorted—or unreasonably negative. Distorted ATs occur so rapidly that we hardly notice them, let alone stop to question them. Yet these ATs profoundly affect our moods and sense of worth. In this section, you'll learn to catch these distortions, challenge their logic, and replace them with thoughts that more closely align with reality instead of thoughts that depress.

The distortions fall into only thirteen categories. Learn them well. Using them will be a very powerful tool in building self-esteem.

Assuming

In some circumstances, we assume the worst without testing the evidence. For instance, in the example above, John assumed that the boss's scowl meant he was angry with John. John could have tested this assumption by simply asking, "Boss, are you angry with me?"

Other examples of assuming self-talk include "I know I won't enjoy myself," or "I know I'll do a lousy job even though I'm prepared." More reasonable self-talk looks like this: "I might or might not enjoy myself (do a good job, and so forth). I'm willing to experiment and see what happens."

Shoulds (Musts and Oughts)

"Shoulds" (including musts and oughts) are demands we make of ourselves. For example, "I should be a perfect lover"; "I must not make mistakes"; "I should have known better"; or "I should be happy and never depressed or tired." We think that we motivate ourselves with such statements. Usually, however, we just feel worse (for example, since I *should* be so-and-so, and I'm not that way, I then feel inadequate, frustrated, ashamed, and hopeless).

Perhaps one of the only reasonable "shoulds" is that humans *should* be fallible, just as we are, given our background, our imperfect understanding, and our present skill levels. If we *really* knew better (that is, if we clearly understood the advantages of certain behaviors, and we were perfectly capable of behaving that way), then we *would* be better. One solution to this thinking, then, is to replace "shoulds" with "woulds" or "coulds" (It *would* be nice if I did that. I wonder how I *could* do that). Or, replace "should" with "want to" (I *want to* do that because it is to my advantage, not because someone is telling me I *should* or *must*).

The Fairy Tale Fantasy

The fairy tale fantasy means demanding the ideal from life. This is really a special type of "should." "That's not fair!" or "Why did that have to happen?" often means "The world shouldn't be the way it is." In reality, bad and unfair things happen to good people—sometimes randomly, sometimes because of the unreasonableness of others, and sometimes because of our own imperfections. To expect the world to be different is to invite disappointment. To expect that others treat us fairly, when they often have their own ideas about what is fair, is also to invite disappointment. Again, a "would" or a "could" is a wise substitute for a "should." (It *would* be nice if things were ideal, but they're not. Too bad. Now, I wonder what I *could* do to improve things.)

All-or-Nothing Thinking

With all-or-nothing thinking you hold yourself to the impossible standard of perfection (or something close to it). When you fall short of this standard, you conclude that you are a total failure as a person. For example, "If I'm not the best, I'm a flop"; "If I'm not performing perfectly, I'm a loser"; "If I score below 90 percent, I am a failure"; "A rough edge means I'm all bad." This type of thinking is unreasonable, because such absolute, black-and-white extremes rarely exist. Even if it were possible to perform perfectly (it isn't), performing below some standard usually means we've performed at 80 percent or 35 percent—rarely at 0 percent. And poor *performance* never makes a complex *person* worthless, just fallible. Ask yourself, "Why *must* I bat one thousand?"

Overgeneralizing

Overgeneralizing is deciding that negative experiences describe your life completely. For example, "I *always* ruin *everything*"; "I *always* get rejected in love"; "*No one* likes me"; "*Everybody* hates me"; "I *never* do well at math." Such global statements are unkind, depressing, and usually inaccurate to some degree. The antidote is to use more precise language: "*Some* of my skills are not *yet* well developed"; "I'm not as tactful in *some* social situations as I'd like to be"; "*Sometimes* people don't approve of me, but *sometimes some* people do"; "Although *some* aspects of my life haven't gone well, that doesn't mean I never do reasonably well." Be a healthy optimist: expect to find small ways to improve situations, and notice what's going well.

Labeling

Sometimes you may give yourself a label or a name, as though a single word describes a person completely. For example, "I'm such a loser"; "I'm stupid"; "I'm dumb"; "I'm boring." To say "I *am* stupid" means I *always*, in every way, am stupid. In fact, some people who behave quite stupidly at times also behave quite intelligently at other times. Because humans are too complex for simple labels, confine labels to behaviors (for example, "That was a silly thing to do."), or ask, "Am I *always* stupid?" Sometimes, perhaps, but not *always*.

Dwelling on the Negative

Suppose you go to a party and notice that a guest has dog poop on his shoe. The more you think about it, the more uncomfortable you get. When you experience this distortion, you focus on the negative aspects of a situation, while ignoring the positive aspects. Soon the whole situation looks negative. Other examples include "How can I feel good about the day now that I have been criticized?" "How can I enjoy life when my children have problems?" "How can I feel good about myself when I make mistakes?" "The steak is burnt—the meal is ruined!" A solution to this habit is to reexamine your options: "Would I enjoy things more, and feel better about myself, if I chose a different focus?" "What pleasing things could I still find to enjoy?" "What would I think on a good day?" "How would someone with sound self-esteem view this situation?"

Rejecting the Positive

The *dwelling on the negative* distortion *overlooks* positive aspects. However, when we reject the positive, we actually *negate* positives so that our self-esteem remains low. For example, let's say someone compliments your work. You reply, "Oh, it was really nothing. Anyone could do that." By saying this, you discount the fact that you've worked long and effectively. It's no wonder accomplishments aren't fun. You could just as easily have replied, "Thanks," and told yourself, "I do deserve special credit for doing this difficult and boring task." You would give a loved one or a friend credit when it's due. Why not do yourself the same favor?

Unfavorable Comparisons

Suppose you had an unusual magnifying glass that magnified some things (like your faults and mistakes, or the strengths of others) and shrunk others (like your strengths, and the mistakes of others). In comparison to others, you would always seem inadequate or inferior—always coming out on the short end of the stick.

For example, you say to a friend, "I'm only a housewife and mother" (minimizing your strengths). "Jan's a rich, bright lawyer" (magnifying another's strengths). Your friend replies, "But you're an excellent homemaker. You've been great with your kids. Jan's an alcoholic." To which you respond, "Yes, but look at the cases she's won!" (minimizing another's faults and your accomplishments). "She's the one who really contributes!" (magnifying another's strengths).

A way to challenge this distortion is to ask, "Why must I compare? Why can't I just appreciate that each person has unique strengths and weaknesses?" Another's contributions are not necessarily better, just different.

Catastrophizing

When you believe that something is a catastrophe, you tell yourself that it is so horrible and awful that you won't be able to *stand* it! By telling ourselves things like this (or, for example, "I couldn't stand it if she were to leave me. It would be awful!"), we convince ourselves that we are too feeble to cope with life. Although many things are unpleasant, inconvenient, and difficult, we really can stand anything short of being steamrolled to death, as Dr. Albert Ellis taught. Instead, you might think, *I don't like this, but I certainly can stand it.*

Asking the following questions will challenge the belief that something will be a catastrophe.

- What are the odds of this happening?

- If it does happen, how likely is it to do me in?

- If the worst happens, what will I do? (Anticipating a problem and formulating an action plan increases one's sense of confidence.)

- One hundred years from now, will anyone care about this?

Personalizing

Personalizing is seeing yourself as more involved in negative events than you really are. For example, a student drops out of college and the mother concludes that it's all her fault. A husband takes full responsibility for his spouse's fatigue or anger, or for a divorce. In these examples the ego is so involved that each event becomes a test of worth. There are two helpful antidotes to this distortion:

1. Distinguish *influences* from *causes*. Sometimes we can influence the decisions of others, but the final decision is theirs, not ours.

2. Look realistically for influences outside of yourself. For example, instead of thinking *What's wrong with me? Why can't I do this?*, one might say, "This is a difficult task. The help I need isn't here, it's noisy, and I'm tired." Instead of thinking *Why is he snapping at me?*, one might say, "Maybe I'm not the central character. Maybe he's mad at the world today."

Blaming

Blaming is the opposite of personalizing. Whereas personalizing puts all the responsibility on yourself for your difficulties, blaming puts it all on something outside of yourself. Consider the following examples:

- He makes me so mad!

- She has ruined my life and my self-esteem.

- I am a loser because of my crummy childhood.

The problem with blaming, much like catastrophizing, is that it tends to make us think of ourselves as helpless victims who are too powerless to cope. The antidote to blaming is to acknowledge outside influences, but to also take responsibility for your own welfare: "Yes, his behavior was unjust and unfair, but I don't have to turn bitter and cynical. I am better than that."

Notice that the person with self-esteem is free to assume realistic responsibility. He will acknowledge what *is* his responsibility and what is *not*. However, when one takes responsibility, it is for a behavior or a choice, not for being bad to the core. Thus, one might say, "I performed poorly on that exam because I did not study enough. Next time I'll plan better." There is no judging the core self here, only behaviors.

Making Feelings Facts

Making feelings facts is taking one's feelings as proof of the way things really are. Consider these examples of distorted thinking:

- I feel like such a loser. I must be hopeless.

- I feel ashamed and bad. I must be bad.

- I feel inadequate. I must be inadequate.

- I feel worthless. I must be worthless.

Remember that feelings result from our thoughts. If our thoughts are distorted (as they often are when we're stressed or depressed), then our feelings may not reflect reality. So question your feelings. Ask, "What would someone who is 100 percent inadequate (or bad, guilty, or hopeless) be like? Am I really like that?" This question challenges our tendencies for labeling or all-or-nothing thinking. Remind yourself that feelings are not facts. When our thoughts become more reasonable, our feelings become brighter.

The Daily Thought Record

Now that you know about distortions, the next step is to use them to help you with your self-esteem. When we're stressed or depressed, thoughts and feelings can swirl in our minds and seem overwhelming. Putting them down on paper helps us sort it all out and see things more clearly. The daily thought record (on the following pages) takes about fifteen minutes each day. It is good to do it after you notice yourself feeling upset. Or you can do it later in the day, when things calm down. Here's how it works.

The Facts

At the top of the record, briefly describe an upsetting event and the resulting feelings (such as sad, anxious, guilty, frustrated). Rate the intensity of these feelings (1 means not at all unpleasant, and 10 means extremely unpleasant). Remember, getting in touch with disturbing feelings is a way to stop them from controlling us.

Analysis of Your Thoughts

In the first column ("initial responses") of the "analysis of your thoughts" section, list your ATs. Then rate how much you believe each one: 1 means not believable at all, and 10 means completely believable.

In the second column, identify the distortions (some ATs might be rational) under "thought fallacies."

In the third column, "reasonable responses," try to respond, or talk back, to each distorted AT. Realize that your first AT is only one of several possible choices. Try to imagine what you would say to a friend who said what you did, or try to imagine yourself on a good day saying something more reasonable. Ask yourself, "What is the evidence for the reasonable response?" Then rate how much you believe each response.

Results

After all this, go back to the "initial responses" column and rerate your ATs. Then at the top, rerate the intensity of your emotions. If the process leads to even a slight drop in your upset feelings, feel satisfied. Even with this process, upsetting events will probably still be upsetting, just not as disturbing.

Remember, work out your thoughts on paper. They are too complex to work out in your head. Be patient with yourself. It usually takes a few weeks to become good at this skill.

Each day for the next two weeks, select an upsetting event and do a daily thought record. At the end of the two weeks, proceed to the next section, "Getting to the Bottom of Things."

Daily Thought Record

Date: _____

The Facts

Event (Describe the event that "made you" feel bad or uncomfortable.)	Impact of Event (Describe the emotions you felt.)	Intensity (Rate the intensity of these emotions from 1–10.)

Analysis of Your Thoughts

Initial Responses (Describe the automatic thoughts or self-talk. Then rate how believable each is from 1–10.)		Thought Fallacies (Find and label the distortions.)	Reasonable Responses (Talk back! Change the distortions to more reasonable thoughts. Rate how much you believe each one from 1–10.)	
	Ratings			Ratings

Results

Based upon your thought analysis, rerate how much you believe your initial responses. Then rerate the intensity of your emotions.

Here's an example of a simplified daily thought record.

Event	Impact	Intensity
Bill and I broke up.	Depressed	9→6
	Worthless	8→5

Analysis

Automatic Thoughts	Ratings	Distortions	Reasonable Responses	Ratings
It's all my fault.	8→5	Feel worthless Personalizing	We both made mistakes, even though we did as well as we were able.	8
I feel so rejected. I'm worthless.	9→8	Making Feelings Facts Labeling	As long as I have ever, or could ever, make a difference to someone (including myself), I'm not worthless.	7
He hates me.	7→3	Assuming	He might just feel that I'm not his cup of tea.	9
I'll never find another as suitable.	10→8	Assuming	I don't know that. It's possible that I could find someone more accepting and, therefore, more suitable.	7
Without him nothing will be fun.	10→5	Assuming	I won't know this unless I test it out. Probably there are things I could enjoy both alone and with others.	7
That guy has ruined my life.	9→5	Blaming	Nobody but me can ruin my life. I'll rebound from this and find ways to enjoy myself.	9

Here is another blank daily thought record to practice on or to copy.

Daily Thought Record

Date: _____

The Facts

Event (Describe the event that "made you" feel bad or uncomfortable.)	Impact of Event (Describe the emotions you felt.)	Intensity (Rate the intensity of these emotions from 1–10.)

Analysis of Your Thoughts

Initial Responses (Describe the automatic thoughts or self-talk. Then rate how believable each is from 1–10.)		Thought Fallacies (Find and label the distortions.)	Reasonable Responses (Talk back! Change the distortions to more reasonable thoughts. Rate how much you believe each one from 1–10.)	
	Ratings			Ratings

Results

Based upon your thought analysis, rerate how much you believe your initial responses. Then rerate the intensity of your emotions.

Getting to the Bottom of Things: The Question and Answer Technique

So far you have learned to use the daily thought record to identify and replace distorted ATs. While replacing distorted ATs can strengthen self-esteem, uprooting core beliefs provides an even greater lift. Core beliefs are deeply held beliefs. Because they are usually learned early in life, they are rarely challenged. We uncover core beliefs by starting with an AT and using the question and answer technique. In this approach, you take an AT and ask the following questions, repeating the last one until you reach the core belief (the last question will usually uncover the core belief):

What does this mean to me?

Assuming that's true, why is that so bad? (or, Why would that be so bad?)

What does that say about me?

For example, on one daily thought record, Jane expressed a feeling of helplessness and worthlessness because her daughter refused to clean her room. Jane decided to apply the question and answer technique to the AT "The room is a mess." The process went like this:

Automatic thought:	The room is a mess.
Question:	What does that mean to me?
Answer:	She's a slob!
Question:	Assuming that's true, why is that so bad?
Answer:	My friends will come over and see her messy room.
Question:	Why would that be so bad?
Answer:	They'll think I'm an inadequate mother.
Question:	What does that say about me?
Answer:	I'm not worthwhile if my friends don't approve of me = *core belief!*

In reaching this core belief, she's assumed that each answer along the way is true. Now go back and look for distortions among your answers, responding reasonably at each step. The following shows what the whole process looks like, using the three columns from the daily thought record. The Q represents questions, which need not be written down.

Initial Responses (ATs)	Distortions	Reasonable Responses
This room is a mess.		
Q		
She's a slob.	Labeling	Actually she's quite neat in areas that matter to her, like her appearance.
Q		
My friends will come over and see her messy room.		Even if they do, lots of worthwhile people have daughters with sloppy rooms.
Q		
They'll think I'm an inadequate mother.	Assuming All-or-nothing thinking	They might just think I'm fallible, just like them.
Q		
I'm not worthwhile if my friends don't approve of me.	*Core belief!*	I don't have to be perfect or have everyone's approval to be happy, or to consider myself worthwhile. It *would* be nice if everything I did was beyond reproach. But since no one is perfect, I'd better decide to feel worthwhile anyway.

Common Core Beliefs

Research has found that a number of core beliefs identified by psychologist Albert Ellis are consistently linked to self-dislike and depression. These deserve special mention, along with their rational replacements (Bourne 1992).

1. **Core belief:** *Everyone I consider significant must love or approve of me.*

    Rational response: I want most people to love or approve of me, and I will try to act in a respectful manner so they will. But it is inevitable that some people, for their own reasons, will not like or accept me. This is not catastrophic; my self-esteem can't depend on the whims of others.

2. **Core belief:** *I must be thoroughly competent and adequate in everything I do. I should not be satisfied with myself unless I'm the best or I'm excelling.*

   Rational response: I will strive to do *my* best rather than to be *the* best. I can enjoy doing things even if I'm not particularly good at them. I'm not afraid to try things that I might fail at; I'm fallible, and failing does not mean I'm a lousy person. Rather, taking risks is courageous and is a necessity if I'm to grow and experience life's opportunities.

3. **Core belief:** *If something may be dangerous or fearsome, I must be terribly concerned about it and keep on guard in case it happens.*

   Rational response: It is probably in my best interest to face this thing and render it less dangerous. If that is impossible, I will at least stop dwelling on it and being fearful. Worry will not stop it from happening. Even if it happens, I can cope with it.

4. **Core belief:** *It is easier to avoid than to face life's difficulties and responsibilities.*

   Rational response: I'll do those necessary things no matter how much I dislike them. Resting and avoiding are often legitimate intervals in a full life, but they are counterproductive if they occupy the major part of my life.

Please note that the last two core beliefs are opposite extremes for dealing with worries. Research shows that such extremes are generally self-defeating. That is, obsessing about worries and denying or avoiding them tend to have negative consequences. As a rule, the middle-ground approach of *efficient* worry has the healthiest consequences: Focus on worries for a limited time, with a problem-solving approach. For a portion of the day (some research suggests about thirty minutes), gather facts, consider alternatives, acknowledge feelings, and write or talk about your concerns. Take appropriate action, and then allow yourself to shift your focus to life's loveliness.

Examining Unproductive Core Beliefs

Below is a list of commonly held, yet unproductive, core beliefs. As an exercise, circle those that you hold. Then try to dispute them. You might further discuss rational responses with a respected friend or mental health professional.

1. It's bad to think well of myself.

2. I can't be happy unless a certain condition—like success, money, love, approval, or perfect achievement—is met.

3. I can't feel worthwhile unless a certain condition is met.

4. I'm entitled to happiness (or success, health, self-respect, pleasure, love) without having to work for it.

5. One day when I make it, I'll have friends and be able to enjoy myself.

6. Work should be hard and in some way unpleasant.

7. Joy is *only* gained from hard work.

8. I am inadequate.

9. Worrying ensures that I'll be prepared to face and solve problems. So the more I worry the better. Constant worrying helps prevent future mistakes and problems and gives me extra control.

10. Life should be easy. I can't enjoy it if there are problems.

11. The past makes me unhappy. There's no way around it.

12. There's a perfect solution, and I must find it.

13. If people disapprove of (reject, criticize, mistreat) me, it means I'm inferior, wrong, or no good.

14. I'm only as good as the work I do. If I'm not productive, I'm no good.

15. If I try hard enough, all people will like me.

16. If I try hard enough, my future will be happy and trouble free.

17. Life must be fair.

Notice how many of these core beliefs directly affect self-esteem! Notice how many of these core beliefs make an external condition a requirement of worth or happiness. For one week, use the question and answer technique once a day to find your core beliefs. Use the distorted automatic thoughts you uncovered in previously completed or newly completed daily thought records.

CHAPTER 6

Acknowledge Reality— "Nevertheless!"

Now that you have acquired the skill of recognizing and replacing self-defeating thoughts, you are ready for a skill that is quite a favorite among students of self-esteem. The appeal of this skill is that it helps one acknowledge reality and still feel good about one's core self.

First, let's review some key points:

1. Feeling bad about events, behaviors, outcomes, or some other external can be appropriate (as in appropriate guilt or disappointment). This is different from the unhealthy tendency to feel bad about the core self (previously described as shame).

2. Saying "I am not quite adequate for the job yet" is quite different from "I'm no good *as a person*." Feeling bad about failing is very different from thinking *I am a failure* at the core.

3. It's okay to judge your behaviors and skills, but not your core, essential self.

A Skill-Building Activity

We want to acknowledge unpleasant external conditions without condemning the core self. People who dislike the self tend to use *because…therefore* thoughts. For example, "*Because* of (some external condition), *therefore* I am no good as a person." Obviously, this thought will erode self-esteem and/or keep it from developing. So we want to avoid *because…therefore* thoughts.

The *nevertheless* skill (Howard 1992) provides a realistic, upbeat, immediate response to unpleasant externals—a response that reinforces one's sense of worth by separating worth from externals. Therefore, instead of having a *because…therefore* thought, generate an *even though…nevertheless* statement. It looks like this:

Even though _____, *nevertheless* _____.
        (some external)   (some statement of worth)

For example:

Even though I botched that project, *nevertheless* I'm still a worthwhile person.

Other *nevertheless* statements (that can follow an *even though* statement) include:

- Nevertheless, I'm still of great worth.

- Nevertheless, I'm still an important and valuable person.

- Nevertheless, my worth is infinite and unchangeable.

A *Nevertheless* Exercise

Get a partner. Ask your partner to say whatever negative things come to mind, be they true or false, such as:

- You really blew it!

- You have a funny nose!

- You mumble when you talk!

- You bug me!

- You're a big dummy!

To each criticism, put your ego on the shelf, and respond with an *even though...nevertheless* statement. You'll probably want to use some of your cognitive therapy skills. For example, if someone labels you "a dummy," you could respond, "Even though I *behave* in dumb ways sometimes, nevertheless..." Author Jack Canfield (1988) is fond of a similar approach, which even a five-year-old child can apply: "No matter what you do or say, I am still a worthwhile person."

Skill-Building Worksheet

1. For each of the next six days, select three events or situations that have the potential to erode self-esteem.

2. In response to each event or situation, create an *even though...nevertheless* statement. Ideally, try to use the statement during the event or situation. However, it's also useful to practice this skill afterward. To reinforce the skill, briefly describe each event or situation in the second column, record the *even though...nevertheless* statement used in the third column, and then describe the effect that saying the statement to yourself had on your feelings.

	Event/Situation	Statement Used	Effect
Day One/Date: 1. 2. 3.			
Day Two/Date: 1. 2. 3.			
Day Three/Date: 1. 2. 3.			
Day Four/Date: 1. 2. 3.			
Day Five/Date: 1. 2. 3.			
Day Six/Date: 1. 2. 3.			

CHAPTER 7

Regard Your Core Worth

Think of what you have rather than of what you lack. Of the things you have, select the best and then reflect how eagerly you would have sought them if you did not have them.

—Marcus Aurelius

The purpose of this chapter is to help you view your core worth accurately. People who lack self-esteem tend to define their worth narrowly, as being conditional on some trait or behavior. As discussed, when they fail to demonstrate this trait or behavior, then their self-esteem is threatened. By contrast, people with self-esteem feel secure in their worth. They realize that many desirable traits and behaviors *express* their worth and serve as *reminders* of their worth. They do not let poor performance in an area define them. As they mature, they learn that humans express themselves in varied and complex ways, and they discover more and more ways by which they express their own core worth.

Patricia Linville (1987), a Yale psychologist, found that people with an intricate, or complex, view of their self also had more resilient self-esteem when they were stressed. For example, the person who sees himself only as a tennis player is more likely to be deflated by losing a tennis game than a person who, with age and experience, has come to see herself as a composite of many traits that are expressed through various roles.

Each person is like a seed of infinite worth: each individual has every trait, in embryo, needed to flower. Those traits can manifest in many different ways. For example, some people express creative talents artistically, some in the ways they solve problems or survive, and others by the way they help people or show compassion. In some, creative talents seem relatively—although never completely—dormant. Nevertheless, each person possesses some form of creativity in embryo. Likewise, each possesses some quantity of every desirable attribute at some level of development. Even a convict is honest *sometimes*. Even a gang leader can be quite creative in his communication or organizational skills (although with self-esteem, the gang leader might be more likely to use these skills for constructive, rather than destructive, purposes).

Each person can be compared to a portrait in various stages of completion. In one person, one area is quite developed and reflects the light in an interesting way. In another, no one area stands out above the rest, but several areas are somewhat developed, forming a unique and interesting pattern. If we look at each portrait through the eyes of an artist, we can relish the unique patterns and possibilities of each human being.

In the following activity, you will more realistically and honestly recognize the value of your core self, and you will see that even now the core self is being expressed in ways that will remind you of your value.

A Skill-Building Activity

This activity consists of three parts. Part I lists a number of personality traits that describe people. Part II allows you to explore traits that are especially important to you. Part III will help you realize how your responses uniquely demonstrate your core worth.

Part I: Personality Traits

For each of the listed personality traits, rate yourself from 0 to 10: 0 means a complete and total absence of this trait (that is, you never demonstrate it in the least degree), and 10 means that this trait is completely developed (that is, you demonstrate it as well as a human being possibly can). Try to be as fair and accurate as you can. Do not inflate or deflate your ratings. Don't worry if you rate yourself higher for some items and lower for others. This is normal. You are not in competition with others. High ratings do not mean more worth. Remember that worth is already a given and is equal for all. In this activity you are just noticing the unique ways that you presently express worth. All of the benefit comes from being objective. Avoid all-or-nothing thinking and overgeneralizing.

Circle the appropriate rating.

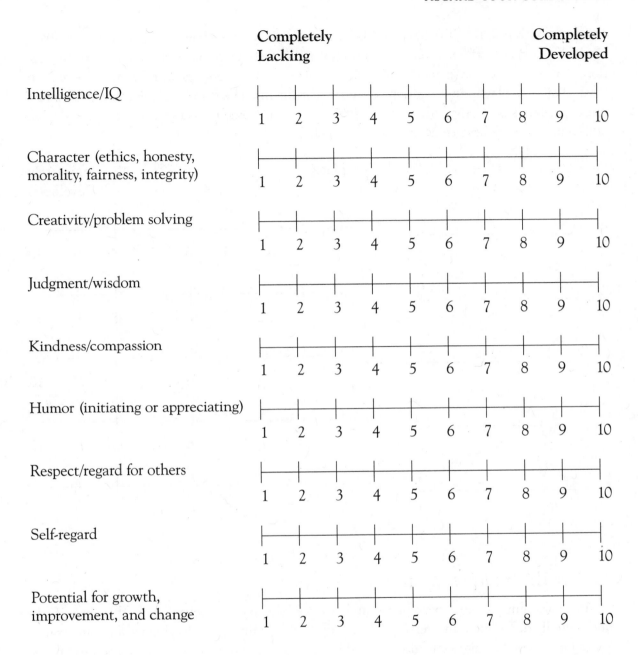

	Completely Lacking									Completely Developed
Intelligence/IQ	1	2	3	4	5	6	7	8	9	10
Character (ethics, honesty, morality, fairness, integrity)	1	2	3	4	5	6	7	8	9	10
Creativity/problem solving	1	2	3	4	5	6	7	8	9	10
Judgment/wisdom	1	2	3	4	5	6	7	8	9	10
Kindness/compassion	1	2	3	4	5	6	7	8	9	10
Humor (initiating or appreciating)	1	2	3	4	5	6	7	8	9	10
Respect/regard for others	1	2	3	4	5	6	7	8	9	10
Self-regard	1	2	3	4	5	6	7	8	9	10
Potential for growth, improvement, and change	1	2	3	4	5	6	7	8	9	10

Part II: Additional Personality Traits

In this part, list five additional traits that describe the way you contribute to the well-being of yourself and/or others. This will not be difficult if you consider the many attributes that describe human beings. Think of Benjamin Franklin's "thirteen virtues" (temperance, silence, order, resolution, frugality, industry, sincerity, justice, moderation, cleanliness, tranquility, chastity, and humility) (Tamarin 1969). Or consider Boy Scout Law (A Scout is trustworthy, loyal…), or other attributes you possess (for example, appreciation, sensitivity, love, introspection, determination, orderliness, warmth, courage, organization, cheer, reverence for human life and dignity, playfulness, gentleness, and discernment). The standard is not that you possess these attributes perfectly, only that you possess them in some measure. Then rate the degree of development of these traits, as you did in part I.

	Completely Lacking									Completely Developed

A. _____

|1|2|3|4|5|6|7|8|9|10|

B. _____

|1|2|3|4|5|6|7|8|9|10|

C._____

|1|2|3|4|5|6|7|8|9|10|

D. _____

|1|2|3|4|5|6|7|8|9|10|

E. _____

|1|2|3|4|5|6|7|8|9|10|

Part III: Interpretation

Because humans are so complex and diverse, the pattern revealed in this exercise is undoubtedly different from everyone else's. You probably rated yourself higher for some traits, lower for others. You probably also noticed an absence of zeroes or tens, since such extremes rarely, if ever, exist.

This activity reveals a complex and unique personal portrait of attributes at various stages of development. Emerging from this composite is a more certain awareness of core worth. The idea of numerical ratings is not to invite comparison with others, but to present an image of wholeness. Core worth is much like a classic painting: Some colors are bright, some are dull. Each complements the others. Together, the colors form a unique whole.

So what about traits with low ratings? There are at least two ways to view these. One is to treasure yourself as you would a beautiful diamond, with its inevitable flaws. Alternatively, you might view traits with lower ratings as areas with the greatest potential for improvement, and savor the challenge.

Please respond to the following questions.

A. As you ponder your responses to parts I and II, which trait(s) do you feel best about?

B. The trait(s) I give myself the most credit for is (are) _____
because…

C. Let's consider the self-as-a-painting analogy. If an impartial observer were to consider the entire portrait, where would "the light shine brightest"? In other words, if a person were to take the time to see you as you really are at present, what areas would this person most likely appreciate or enjoy?

D. From this activity, I learned that…

CHAPTER 8

Create the Habit of Core-Affirming Thoughts

> Self-acceptance does not breed complacence. On the contrary, kindness, respect, encouragement, support, firm but caring discipline…these are the soil and climate for development.
>
> —Anonymous

People with and without self-esteem are fallible. They both make mistakes and fall short of goals and dreams. Both groups include people who are attractive, and some who are not. Both groups include people who have succeeded in business, school, sports, relationships, or other areas, and some who have not. What separates the two groups?

Research and clinical experience indicate that those with self-esteem think about and talk to themselves differently than those who do not have self-esteem. For example, upon failing, those without self-esteem (including people with type A personality and/or high test anxiety) are very self-critical, thinking thoughts like *What's wrong with me? I should have known better! Why am I so dumb?* Such self-rejecting statements further degrade self-esteem. Conversely, those with self-esteem (including people with type B personality and/or low test anxiety) tend to appraise failure more compassionately, focusing on external factors and behaviors (for example, *This test was hard; I had too many other demands on my time; I didn't study enough—I'll prepare better next time*). Such statements tend to preserve self-esteem in the face of stressful situations, enabling one to improve behavior without self-condemnation.

By focusing on what is "wrong" with themselves, people without self-esteem feel deficient and inadequate. They become defeated, losing motivation and the joy of experiencing oneself as worthwhile. If they do push themselves to grow, they do so with perfectionistic standards, in a driven and joyless fashion that paradoxically impairs success (Burns 1980). In contrast, people with self-esteem acknowledge the rightness of the core, despite its rough edges and imperfections. By focusing on what is right, they motivate themselves to grow using a carrot, not a stick.

Cognitive therapy removes the negative thoughts that undermine self-esteem. The activity below is practice for thinking the uplifting and self-affirming thoughts that build and preserve self-esteem.

A Skill-Building Activity

Here is a list of statements representing the dialogue that people with self-esteem typically have with themselves.

1. I think well of myself. This is good.

2. I accept myself because I realize that I am more than my foibles, mistakes, or any other externals.

3. Criticism is an external. I examine it for ways to improve, without concluding that the criticism makes me less worthwhile as a person.

4. I can criticize my own behavior without questioning my worth as a human being.

5. I notice and enjoy each sign of achievement or progress, no matter how insignificant it may seem to myself or others.

6. I enjoy the achievements and progress that others make, without concluding they are more valuable than I am as a person.

7. I am generally capable of living well, and of applying the time, effort, patience, training, and assistance needed to do so.

8. I expect others to like and respect me. If they don't, that's okay.

9. I can usually earn people's trust and affection through sincere and respectful treatment. If not, that's okay.

10. I generally show sound judgment in relationships and work.

11. I can influence others by my well-reasoned viewpoints, which I can present and defend effectively.

12. I like to help others enjoy themselves.

13. I enjoy new challenges and don't get upset when things don't go well right off the bat.

14. The work I do is generally of good quality, and I expect to do many worthwhile things in the future.

15. I am aware of my strengths and respect them.

16. I can laugh at some of the ridiculous things I do sometimes.

17. I can make a difference in people's lives by what I contribute.

18. I enjoy making others feel happier and glad for time we shared.

19. I consider myself a worthwhile person.

20. I like being a one-of-a-kind portrait. I'm glad to be unique.

21. I like myself without comparison to others.

22. I feel stable and secure inside because I regard rightly my core worth.

Now, using the statements above, do the following activity.

1. Sit in a quiet place, well supported in a chair, where you will be comfortable for about twenty minutes.

2. Close your eyes. Take two deep breaths and relax your body as deeply and as completely as possible. Prepare yourself for, and expect, a pleasant experience.

3. Open your eyes long enough to read the first statement. Then close your eyes and *concentrate* on that statement. Repeat it to yourself three times slowly, allowing yourself to feel as though the statement is completely accurate. You may try imagining yourself in a situation in which you actually think and believe the statement. Use all your senses to experience the situation.

4. Don't worry if a statement doesn't seem to apply to you yet. Just think of this as patient practice for creating a new mental habit. Don't allow negative or pessimistic thoughts to distract you or undermine your progress. Accept whatever actually happens, without demanding perfection. If a statement does not feel right, bypass it and return to it later. Or modify it so that it does feel right; be sure to keep it positive.

5. Repeat step 3 for each statement. The entire exercise will take about twenty minutes.

6. Repeat this activity each day for six days.

7. Each day, after doing this activity, notice how you feel. Many notice that with practice the thoughts begin to feel more and more comfortable, becoming as trusted friends. Thoughts that do not become comfortable within six days will likely become so when you return to them after completing the rest of this workbook.

CHAPTER 9

An Overview of Unconditional Human Worth

So far, we have explored some very important ideas and skills related to the first building block of self-esteem, unconditional human worth. Because future ideas and skills will build on these pillars, it is important to pause and review what we have learned thus far.

Three Important Ideas

1. Each person is of infinite, unchanging, and equal worth, which comes with birth.

2. The core self is separate from externals. Externals can cover up the core, or help it to shine, but the worth of the core is constant.

3. People express their worth in unique ways and patterns, but each person, at the core, is whole, possessing all necessary attributes in embryo.

Four Learned Skills

1. Replace negative, core-attacking thoughts called distortions.

2. Use the *even though…nevertheless* skill.

3. Regard your core worth.

4. Create the habit of thinking core-affirming thoughts.

General Review

It is helpful to reinforce the ideas and skills you learned in the previous chapters. Therefore, please take a few moments to complete the following statements. You might first wish to flip back through the preceding pages to review what you've done.

The ideas that have had the most meaning to me are...

The skills that I would most like to remember are...

I am always grateful for the way the universe provides clarifying moments and insights. The following, by American suffragette Elizabeth Cady Stanton, was posted at a bed-and-breakfast:

> I thought that the chief thing to be done in order to equal boys was to be learned and courageous. So I decided to study Greek and learn to manage a horse.

The proprietress of the bed-and-breakfast, a wonderful woman, skilled with horses, noticed me reading the posting and said, "Isn't that a wonderful quote?" "Yes," I said, "I wrote it down. But it makes me somewhat uncomfortable." "Why?" she asked. "I love the way managing a horse gives me a sense of control."

"I agree," said I. "It's a good thing to be learned and courageous. But the underlying proposition is all wrong, that one must do something to be equal—that is, of equal worth—with another. It is good to do these things because they are satisfying, but not to be equal to anybody else. We already are."

FACTOR II

Experiencing Unconditional Love

CHAPTER 10

The Basics of Unconditional Love

Earlier I posed this question: How does one build self-esteem in the absence of parental antecedents? So far, we have explored the first building block, or factor, of building self-esteem: unconditional human worth. This factor is based on one's accurate recognition of core worth. As such, this factor relates to cognition, or the intellect.

Factor II, unconditional love, is a beautiful and extremely powerful building block that primarily concerns emotions. Whereas factor I primarily concerns the *realistic* part of the definition of self-esteem, factor II primarily relates to the *appreciative* part of the definition. Let us now turn our attention to this factor.

Unlike unconditional human worth, a cognition which one thinks about, love is something you experience. Although philosophers like to intellectualize it, people recognize love when they see it. Have you ever known anyone who didn't?

When Mother Teresa ministered to people, whether it was a dying man in Calcutta or a spastic child in Lebanon, something fascinating happened. At the moment they looked into her eyes and felt great love coming through them, they no longer looked away. They became calmer, and their countenance softened. Did they think, *Hmmmm…let's see, is this* agape, eros, *or filial love?* No. They simply recognized love and responded to it. They felt it by the way she looked at them, spoke to them, and touched them (Petrie and Petrie 1986).

Basic Principles

1. Each person has been created to love and be loved, as Mother Teresa observed (Petrie and Petrie 1986).

2. Each person needs affirming, or love, to *feel* like somebody of worth. That is, everybody needs a source to affirm that they are loved, accepted, and worthwhile. As the

psychologist Abraham Maslow (1968) said, "The need for love characterizes every human being that is born…. No psychological health is possible unless the essential core…is…accepted, loved and respected." Thus, love is important. If you have not received it from others, it is good to provide it for yourself.

What Is Love?

It helps to have a clear understanding of the nature of love, which is the second factor of self-esteem and an important building block. Love is:

1. A *feeling* that you *experience*. One recognizes it when one sees it.

2. An *attitude*. Love wants what's best for the loved one at each moment. (Please note: Love for others and love for self are not mutually exclusive. Ideally, the attitude of loving encircles both.)

3. A *decision* and a commitment that you make every day. Sometimes you "will it," even though this may be difficult at times.

4. A *skill* that is cultivated.

Some mistakenly assume that love—and related feelings like appreciation, acceptance, and affection—is only a feeling that we either have or we don't. This simplistic view overlooks the notion that love is also an act of will and a skill. Although anyone can recognize and respond to love, loving is something that we learn to do.

Television's Mr. (Fred) Rogers demonstrated unconditional love daily, telling children, "I like you just the way you are." He sang the following song (Rogers 1970) on his show. Notice the messages of separating worth from externals, and of liking the core.

It's you I like,
It's not the things you wear,
It's not the way you do your hair—
But it's you I like.
The way you are right now,
The way down deep inside you—
Not the things that hide you.

Mr. Rogers was a sickly child, confined during ragweed season to the only room in his house with an air conditioner. At eight years of age, he visited his grandfather's farm. He rejoiced as he scrambled along the stone walls of the farm. Afterward, his grandfather told him, "Fred, you made this day special by being yourself. Remember, there's just one person in the world like you, and I like you just the way you are" (Sharapan 1992).

This story demonstrates that we each stand on the shoulders of those who have gone before us, and that *loving unconditionally is learned*.

Two Stories of Love

It is easier to recognize love than to define it. The following two stories depict love nicely.

Love Finds a Way

When seventy-year-old Bernie Meyers of Wilmette, Illinois, died suddenly of cancer, his ten-year-old granddaughter Sarah Meyers didn't have a chance to say good-bye to him. For weeks Sarah said little about what she was feeling. But then one day she came home from a friend's birthday party with a bright-red helium balloon. "She went into the house," her mother recalls, "and came out carrying the balloon—and an envelope addressed to 'Grandpa Bernie, in Heaven Up High.'"

The envelope contained a letter in which Sarah told her grandfather that she loved him and hoped somehow he could hear her. Sarah printed her return address on the envelope, tied the envelope to the balloon and let it go. "The balloon seemed so fragile," her mother remembers. "I didn't think it would make it past the trees. But it did."

Two months passed. Then one day a letter arrived addressed to "Sarah Meyers Family" and bearing a York, Pennsylvania, postmark.

> Dear Sarah, Family & Friends: Your letter to Grandpa Bernie Meyers apparently reached its destination and was read by him. I understand they can't keep material things up there, so it drifted back to Earth. They just keep thoughts, memories, love, and things like that. Sarah, whenever you think about your grandpa, he knows and is very close by with overwhelming love. Sincerely, Don Kopp (also a grandpa).

Kopp, a sixty-three-year-old retired receiving clerk, had found the letter and the nearly deflated balloon while hunting in northeastern Pennsylvania—almost six hundred miles from Wilmette. The balloon had floated over at least three states and one of the Great Lakes before coming to rest on a blueberry bush.

"Though it took me a couple of days to think of what to say," Kopp notes, "it was important to me that I write to Sarah."

Says Sarah, "I just wanted to hear from Grandpa somehow. In a way, now I think I *have* heard from him."

—Bob Greene in the *Chicago Tribune* (1990)

Learning About Love: A Story About Mother Teresa

My own mother…used to be very busy the whole day, but as soon as the evening [came], she used to move very fast to get ready to meet my father. At that time we didn't understand; we used to laugh; and we used to tease her; but now I remember what a tremendous, delicate love she had for him. Didn't matter what happened, but she was ready there with a smile to meet him.

—Quoted in D. S. Hunt, *Love: A Fruit Always in Season*

Sources of Love

Love can be experienced from at least three sources: parents, self, and significant others. Theologians add an important fourth source, divine love. Most theologies teach that God's love is unconditional, a gift of grace, always accessible, and the securest foundation for growth. This spiritual foundation can be vitally useful, although a full exploration of God's love is beyond the scope of this book.

Parents

Parents are an ideal source of unconditional love. Although it would be nice if you received unconditional love from your folks, parents are fallible people who love imperfectly. No children received perfect unconditional love from their parents. It does no good to waste time begrudging the love that you did not receive in the past. As we discussed earlier in the book, blaming keeps you stuck in the past, and it contributes to your feeling that you are a helpless victim.

Self

If one has not received love from others, one could ask, "How can I furnish the love I need to flourish?" One can provide this needed love in many ways, as we will soon see.

Significant Others

The love of significant others, such as friends, spouses, or relatives, is intentionally listed as the last resource. It is nice to receive love from others; however, as with parents, others will never provide perfect unconditional love. The reaction we get from others is more likely to be a reflection of how they feel about themselves than a true reflection of our core worth. When people lack a realistic, appreciative opinion of themselves, they often become socially needy. That is, they turn to others for the approval—of their core—that they themselves lack and so desperately want. They can smother others and suck them emotionally dry. When their insecurity drives people away, the rejection is devastating. Even if they win the esteem of others, this is *other*-esteem, not *self*-esteem. The esteem of others is no substitute for the inner security of self-esteem.

So the prudent course is to first be responsible for the source of love that you can depend on: you. Before exploring ways to furnish wholesome love, let's explore some important additional premises regarding love.

Additional Premises Regarding Love

Like worth, love must be unconditional, unshaken by temporary defeats, and independent of daily self-evaluations. In other words, one might say to oneself, "Even though I am performing poorly, I still love me."

Love also makes you *feel* like somebody. It doesn't define you or provide your worth. It just helps you realize, experience, and appreciate it. Perhaps you've heard the beautiful old melody "You're Nobody till Somebody Loves You." With no disrespect meant to the songwriters, the song might better be entitled, "You're Always a Somebody, and Love Helps You *Know* It!"

Lastly, love is the foundation for growth. The reverse is rarely true. Hence, producing or overachieving usually does not fill the painful void that lack of love for the core self creates. Ted Turner, Gloria Steinem, and astronaut Buzz Aldrin are a few examples of people who succeeded brilliantly in producing and achieving, but each realized later in life that something was missing *inside*. That something is a genuine feeling of affection for the core self. This affection is the soil and climate of human growth.

A number of authors have stated that people cannot love others if they do not love the self, and that even genuine, mature love from another cannot reverse self-dislike. Personally, I wonder if that is an overstatement. I think that genuine, mature love from others can and does change one's self-concept. It is simply that one cannot always rely on the love of others. And if one is fortunate enough to find it, there is no *guarantee* that another's love alone will change self-dislike. So we return to the one area that a person can take full responsibility for, the self.

Dr. Joseph Michelotti's (1991) parents were immigrants from a small Italian farm. They raised six children; one became a physicist, while others became doctors and lawyers. The children were raised with great love. His mother, especially, seemed to understand the value of the core self. Musing over her favorite portrait, she commented that when you died, "God gave you back your 'best self'... This is what I'm going to look like in heaven." When Joseph was older, she told him, "You don't have to buy me a birthday present. Instead write me a letter about yourself. Tell me about your life. Is anything worrying you? Are you happy?"

In high school, Joseph tried to discourage his parents from coming to watch him play in the orchestra for *The Music Man*. He reasoned that his role was unimportant. "Nonsense," she replied. "Of course we're coming, and we're coming because you're in the program." The whole family showed up. Great love, encouragement, and expectations for the betterment of mankind...a fine formula for building self-esteem. If you didn't receive these things from loved ones, then it is good to provide them for yourself.

Reflections on Love

Before moving on to the next chapter, please consider the following reflections on love.

Each individual person has been created to love and be loved.
There is a hunger greater than the hunger for bread...the hunger for love.
Small things with great love. It's not how much we do—but how much love we put in the doing, and it is not how much we give—but how much love we put in the giving.

—Mother Teresa

A human being's first responsibility is to shake hands with himself.

—Henry Winkler

CHAPTER 11

Find, Love, and Heal the Core Self

If you didn't have loving parents, then you had better learn to be a loving parent to yourself.

—Anonymous

Life is not about pedestals and power. Life is about love. As Mother Teresa said, each person "has been created to love and be loved." It is love that really heals, not so much the intellect, although cognition supports the process.

In a sense, love is the foundation of effective stress management because it is the foundation of mental health and self-esteem. Stress management is really about managing life. It offers skills to help one cope in the present, but it largely ignores the power of healing the past so that we can enjoy the present. Studies (Pennebaker 1997; Borkovec et al. 1983) have shown that writing about one's past and present worries greatly improves the mood and the immune system.

There are various theories advanced to explain these results. Some think that putting pent-up worries or traumas on paper releases and discharges them, providing great relief. Some think that in writing about such concerns people gain distance, objectivity, perspective, and sometimes solutions. Personally, I think that there is another reason: Writing about feelings acknowledges and honors those feelings, which are typically disowned in shame-based people (that is, people who feel bad to the core). Writing about your feelings is a way of loving yourself.

Love Heals the Child Within Us

There is within each of us a light...a core of peace, wholeness, joy, goodness, innate worth, and feelings that are good and that make us human. This core being is sometimes metaphorically called the "inner child." The inner child possesses, in embryo, every attribute it needs, plus the inborn tendency to grow and polish the rough edges.

With time, however, we usually—to one degree or another—separate or split from the inner child. We understand this process well: abuse, abandonment, criticism, and/or neglect interact with personal fallibilities and choices, leading people to conclude that they are defective and flawed as individuals. They don't believe that they *make* mistakes, but instead that they *are* a mistake, bad at the core. Thus, the core inner child becomes covered, rejected, disowned, split off, or separated. This is the root of self-dislike and shame-based behaviors that are common to so many stress-related dysfunctions.

The truth, however, is that the inner child—though battered, covered, and split off—survives intact. The child you once were, you still are (Leman and Carlson 1989). Our goal as humans is to achieve the healing, integration, wholeness, and reunion of our present consciousness with our inner core of light. The cure, quite simply, is love. We may not call it love in the helping professions, but it is love. Love heals and provides the foundation for growth. Although the adult operates logically, the core inner child hungers for love and continues to cry out until that hunger is touched.

Adults understand this process well. In one of the stress classes I teach, we discuss parenting styles as they relate to stress. I'll ask if any of the students had perfect parents. After a little laughter, I'll ask if anyone had parents who were reasonably close to perfection. Among those who respond, there is usually a look of joy on their faces as they relate how feelings were expressed and respected, and how time and affection were freely given. Typically, these students are doing well in school and life, and they are not neurotically driven individuals. By contrast, those whose need for love has not yet been touched are more likely to experience insecurity, joyless striving, social neediness, anger, and status concern.

Corrective Experiences Repair Early Wounds

The question is, can the adult heal the "hole in the soul" if love was in short supply developmentally? The answer is yes. One approach comes from literature about alcoholism and dysfunctional family life. This literature uses imagery that emphasizes affect coupled with reason. Since many people had imperfect pasts, corrective experiences can settle the past so we can move ahead (Alexander 1932). Below are the instructions for two corrective experiences, adapted from the works of John Bradshaw (1988) and Pam Levin (1988).

Corrective Experience No. 1: Find and Love the Core Self

The purpose of this five-step exercise is to find and love your core self, or your inner child.

1. First, write down the names of your most cherished friends, family members, and/or loved ones, people you feel or felt good to be with; people who make or made you feel warm, safe, accepted, and loved. First identify couples, and then individuals (including friends, colleagues, and teachers).

2. Find a place to sit quietly and comfortably where you won't be disturbed for about fifteen minutes.

3. Take two very deep breaths, saying the word "relax" as you breathe out.

4. Imagine yourself as an infant, surrounded by loving people. These can be the loving people you identified, or two warm, loving grown-ups. You can imagine parents, as you would have liked your parents to ideally have been. Perhaps you imagine composite figures of people you have known and loved, who made you feel like a somebody—a person of worth.

5. As an infant you needed to hear the words in the list below. Imagine yourself hearing these statements, alternately from each person.

   - We're so glad you're here.
   - Welcome to the world.
   - Welcome to our family and home.
   - We're so glad you're a boy (or a girl).
   - You're beautiful.
   - All our children are beautiful.
   - We want to be near you, to hold you, and to love you.
   - Sometimes you'll feel joy and laughter, sometimes sadness and pain and anger and worry. These feelings are all okay with us.
   - We'll be here for you.
   - We'll give you all the time you need to get your needs met.
   - It's okay to wander and separate and explore and experiment.
   - We won't leave you.

   Imagine the speakers of these words cradling you, loving you, and gently gazing upon you with eyes of love as you respond to these feelings.

   Practice this imagery for two consecutive days before continuing to the next corrective experience.

Corrective Experience No. 2: Embracing Your Lost Inner Child

Again, find a place where you can reflect, undisturbed, for at least fifteen minutes. Relax and focus on your breathing for a few minutes. Being mindful of your breathing, be aware of the air as you breathe in and as you breathe out. Notice the difference in the air as you inhale and exhale. Focus on the difference. Now imagine the following, using masculine or feminine pronouns as appropriate:

You are walking down a long flight of stairs. Walk down the stairs slowly and count down from ten to one. When you reach the bottom of the stairs, turn left and walk down a long corridor with doors on your right and doors on your left. Each door has a colored symbol on it. As you look toward the end of the corridor, you'll notice there is a force field of light. Walk through the light and go back through time to a street where you lived before you were seven years old. Walk down that street to the house in which you lived. Look at the house. Notice the roof, the color of the house, and the windows and doors. See a small child come out the front door. How is the child dressed? What color are the child's shoes?

Walk over to the child. Tell her that you are from her future. Tell her that you know better than anyone what she has been through. Her suffering, her abandonment, her shame. Tell her that of all the people she will ever know, you are the only one she will never lose. Now ask her if she is willing to go home with you. If not, tell her you will visit her tomorrow. If she is willing to go with you, take her by the hand and start walking away. Feel the warmth and the joy of that tiny hand and of being with that little person. As you walk away, see your mom and dad come out on the porch. Wave good-bye to them. Look over your shoulder as you continue walking away, and see your parents becoming smaller and smaller until they are completely gone.

Turn the corner and see your higher power and your most cherished friends waiting for you. Embrace all your friends and allow your higher power to come into your heart. See them all embracing the child with joy. Embrace your child and feel her warmly embrace you. Hold the child in your hand and let her shrink to the size of your hand. Or, embrace the child and feel her be absorbed into you, filling you with all her joy, hope, and potential. Tell her that you're placing her in your heart so you can always carry her with you. Promise her you'll meet her for five minutes each day. Pick an exact time. Commit to that time.

Next, imagine that you walk to some beautiful outdoor place. Stand in the middle of that place and reflect on the experience you just had. Get a sense of communion within yourself, with your higher power, and with all things. Now look up at the sky; see the purple-white clouds form the number five. See the five become a four, be aware of your feet and legs. See the four become a three, feel the life in your stomach and in your arms. See the three become a two, feel the life in your hands, your face, and your whole body. Know that you are about to be fully awake—able to do all things with your fully awake mind. See the two become a one and be fully awake, remembering this experience.

Get an early photo of yourself, if you can, to remind yourself of the child who lives within you. Practice this imagery for two consecutive days.

I often ask students to locate and bring an early photo of themselves to class, which they usually do with exquisite pleasure. I remember one student, in particular, whom I was having a difficult time understanding and liking. He was silent and withdrawn and looked down when spoken to. Then he brought in a photo. He was standing as a child beside his immigrant parents. He had the pure and innocent look that only a small and sensitive child can have. From that time on I felt a great affection for that student and saw him through different eyes, eyes that understood his inner self. The true, likable self usually shows through in the child, before externals cover the core. To see the core is to be reminded of the miracle that is each person.

Reprinted with the permission of Jennifer Berman. Copyright 1989 by Jennifer Berman.

CHAPTER 12

The Language of Love

Loving relationships that last are characterized by appreciation, liking, respect, and acceptance. In healthy relationships, there seems to be this unspoken thought: *You know, I realized a long time ago that you are not perfect, not exactly what I expected. I might laugh with you about some of your preferences and idiosyncrasies, but you know that underneath the humor is genuine liking. And I'll never speak to you with contempt or ridicule.* This atmosphere of respect, paradoxically, allows people to change and grow, if they choose to. Similarly, an attitude of kindness toward oneself also encourages and sustains growth.

We have seen how a negative internal dialogue can sabotage growth and life enjoyment. The skills to follow reinforce the decision to think of ourselves realistically *and* kindly.

Kind Descriptions

Do you think of yourself as competent? Does this question prompt you to think, *Well, competent means perfectly competent. I'm certainly not perfectly competent. So I guess, in truth, I must be incompetent?*

This example of black-and-white thinking explains why it is difficult for many people to think well of themselves. Diagrammed, the thought process looks like this:

0 ——— 10

Incompetent   Competent

Here, competent suggests "perfect competence," while incompetent means "without any ability," and "totally unfit." By this line of thinking, if a person is not a 10, he or she must be a 0. In chapter 6 I suggested a way to rate behavior without rating the self. Here is another way to think of the self that is accurate and kind:

|———————————————————|———————————————————|
Incompetent   Competent   Perfect

This way of thinking accurately acknowledges the middle ground. Of course, no one is perfect, which means completed and without flaw. Each person, however, is competent in the relative sense—competent at times and in unique ways, and possessing competence at some incomplete stage of development. By this standard, each person can be considered competent.

At the left end of the continuum below is a list of negative labels. At the polar opposite is perfection. In the middle are kinder, more accurate descriptions of people.

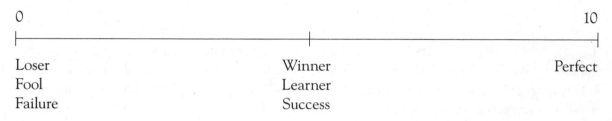

0   10

|———————————————————|———————————————————|
Loser   Winner   Perfect
Fool   Learner
Failure   Success

A "failure" is a person who is defeated without contributing or learning. Because anyone who is still alive is still learning and capable of contributing, then no one needs to conclude that he or she is a failure. If a "success" is one who learns, tries, and contributes at some level, then it is realistic for everyone to think of themselves as successful. This is not an argument for complacency. People can still aim for excellence and for doing their best without demanding perfection.

As an exercise, add some additional labels to the list below. In the center, write a kinder, more accurate description than the word to the left.

0   10

|—————————————————————|—————————————————————|

                                                            Perfect

Idiot   _____

Zero   _____

Noncontributor   _____

Unlikable   _____

_____   _____

_____   _____

_____   _____

Changing Channels

Below are listed some examples of the X-rated self-talk and comments that we speak to ourselves and others—"X-rated" meaning language that demeans and degrades. When you notice yourself thinking or making such comments, it is wise to immediately tell yourself "Stop!" And then change channels. *"Changing channels"* simply means thinking and speaking about yourself respectfully—in ways that encourage growth and build self-esteem. Notice the emotional shift that occurs when you change channels.

X-Rated Self-Talk	Stop! Change Channels
I'm only/just a _____ (teacher, nurse, etc.).	I am a _____ (teacher, nurse, etc.).
	I am an honest, hardworking _____.
	I find satisfaction in being a _____.
	I am looking to advance.
I'll never succeed.	Success is exerting effort, and moving in the desired direction.
If only I'd _____.	Next time I'll…
I hate this about me!	What an interesting quirk!
	I'm going to work on this.
	I'll feel even better about myself as I improve.
I'll probably blow this.	I'm not afraid to try, because my worth comes from within.
I am fat.	I have extra weight. I am working on this extra weight.

X-Rated Self-Surveillance: An Exercise

Walking to class one day, I noticed a graduate student at a picnic table, deep in thought as she worked on this assignment. I quietly walked behind her and "snatched" her purse. As I walked away, I said loudly enough for her to hear, "Boy! That was easy. I hope there's lots of money in this purse." She laughed and turned red. She could have thought *I am so out of it…I am such a space cadet*. Later she showed me what she had written. The assignment said, "I concentrate well despite distractions like purse snatchers." A loving attitude truly is a decision that we make every day. When we choose a loving attitude, the desired feelings eventually follow.

For the next two days, see if you can catch yourself making self-degrading comments. When you do, replace them with encouraging statements.

X-Rated Self-Talk	**Encouraging Comments/Thoughts**
First day	
1.	
2.	
Second day	
1.	
2.	

CHAPTER 13

The Appreciative Opinion of Others

We can make quiet but more honest inventories of our strengths, since, in this connection, most of us are dishonest bookkeepers and need confirming "outside auditors."

—Neal A. Maxwell

It is appropriate, and may be useful, at this juncture to summarize two key points about the love and approval of others.

1. The love and approval of others do not equal self-esteem. Otherwise, it would be called *other*-esteem, not self-esteem.

2. The love and approval of others, however, can aid the growth of self-esteem.

Just as criticism does not damage self-esteem without your consent, love and approval will not build self-esteem without your consent. This is not to discount the preciousness of intimacy; it's only to say that self-esteem is just that: *self*-esteem. If someone loves you and helps you to *feel* like a somebody, this is a wonderful gift for which you can be grateful; however, you can still have self-esteem in the absence of intimacy. For example, a widow living alone can have self-esteem.

Ask yourself, "What do I like about myself? What traits, attributes, skills, contributions, and so forth, do I appreciate?" Many, especially those with little self-esteem and those without practice, will find it difficult to answer these questions.

In the next chapter, you will make an honest inventory of your strengths. The exercise below can assist this process and serve as a warm-up. This exercise assumes that (1) you can assemble a small group of people who know you and each other reasonably well, and that (2) group members are willing to anonymously share their favorable impressions of each other in return for a very enjoyable experience. This exercise will take about an hour, depending on the number of people in the group.

The Circle of Differing Gifts: An Exercise

Approval and affirming words from others do not equal self-esteem. However, allowing the good opinions of others in and examining the opinions can help open our eyes to the truth. This can help stimulate a realistic, appreciative view of self that recognizes one's gifts.

1. Sit in a circle. Six to ten people are ideal, but any number can work. Each person has a pen or pencil and sheet of paper.

2. Each person writes his or her own name on the top of the sheet of paper in large letters.

3. When the signal "pass" is given, people pass the paper to the person sitting to their right.

4. The person who receives the paper proceeds to write three things that he or she appreciates about the person whose name appears on the paper. Entries could include qualities, strengths, attributes, and contributions (for example, "I like your smile"; "I like the way you appreciate and draw my attention to the beauty of nature"; "I appreciate the way you express gratitude"; "You make me feel…"). Scatter your comments around the paper so that no one knows who wrote them.

5. When everyone has completed writing three appreciation items, the signal "ready, pass" is given, whereupon each person passes the sheet to the person on the right. Each person then repeats the instructions for step 4.

6. Continue passing the papers until each sheet has been completed and is in the hands of the person sitting to the left of whomever the sheet belongs to.

7. At this point, each person in turn reads the comments about the person on his or her right. Be sure when you are the listener that you

   - relax;

   - listen, enjoy, and allow each statement to sink in;

   - give people credit for exercising good judgment regarding their comments about you; and

   - do not discount compliments with degrading self-talk (for example, "Yes, but if they only knew"; "They're just being polite"; "I sure snowed them."). If such comments arise, think *Stop! What's happening here is healthy. I'll allow for the possibility that there is some or much truth to these comments.*

The "circle of differing gifts" is a wonderful exercise for people of all ages. It is a wonderful activity for families. Often, you'll hear comments like, "I never knew people thought such things." Good feelings among group members increase. Individuals enjoy keeping their own sheets of paper and referring to them when they need an emotional lift or a reminder of their strengths.

CHAPTER 14

Acknowledge and Accept Positive Qualities

I am larger, better than I thought.
I did not know I held so much goodness.

—Walt Whitman

Self-esteem can be cultivated by resolutely acknowledging what is presently "right" about one's self. For many, this is difficult because habits of negative thinking make it easier to identify what's wrong. Although there is benefit to acknowledging shortcomings and weaknesses, when doing so becomes the dominant focus—to the exclusion of strengths—self-esteem suffers.

The exercise below, then, is practice in acknowledging and reinforcing strengths with appreciation. Doing so is a way of loving yourself. This skill is based on the research of three Canadians, Gauthier, Pellerin, and Renaud (1983), whose method enhanced the self-esteem of subjects in just a few weeks.

To warm up, place a check if you sometimes are, or have been, reasonably:

- ☐ Clean
- ☐ Handy
- ☐ Literate (Come on! If you've read this far, check this.)
- ☐ Punctual
- ☐ Assured or self-confident
- ☐ Enthusiastic or spirited
- ☐ Optimistic
- ☐ Humorous, mirthful, or amusing
- ☐ Friendly
- ☐ Gentle
- ☐ Loyal or committed
- ☐ Trustworthy
- ☐ Trusting, or seeing the best in others
- ☐ Loving
- ☐ Strong, powerful, or forceful
- ☐ Determined, resolute, or firm
- ☐ Patient
- ☐ Rational, reasonable, or logical
- ☐ Intuitive, or trusting of one's own instincts
- ☐ Creative or imaginative
- ☐ Compassionate, kind, or caring
- ☐ Disciplined
- ☐ Persuasive
- ☐ Talented
- ☐ Cheerful
- ☐ Sensitive or considerate
- ☐ Generous

- ☐ Appreciative
- ☐ Respectful or polite
- ☐ Responsive to beauty or nature
- ☐ Principled or ethical
- ☐ Industrious
- ☐ Responsible or reliable
- ☐ Organized, orderly, or neat
- ☐ Sharing
- ☐ Encouraging or complimentary
- ☐ Attractive
- ☐ Well-groomed
- ☐ Physically fit
- ☐ Intelligent or perceptive
- ☐ Cooperative
- ☐ Forgiving, or able to look beyond mistakes or shortcomings
- ☐ Conciliatory
- ☐ Tranquil or serene
- ☐ Successful
- ☐ Open-minded
- ☐ Tactful
- ☐ Spontaneous
- ☐ Flexible or adaptable
- ☐ Energetic
- ☐ Expressive
- ☐ Affectionate
- ☐ Graceful or dignified
- ☐ Adventurous

Check the words that describe what you are sometimes reasonably good at:

☐ Socializing

☐ Listening

☐ Cooking

☐ Athletics

☐ Cleaning

☐ Working

☐ Being a friend

☐ Playing an instrument or singing

☐ Learning

☐ Leading or coaching

☐ Organizing

☐ Making decisions

☐ Counseling

☐ Helping

☐ "Cheerleading" or supporting

☐ Planning

☐ Following

☐ Correcting mistakes

☐ Smiling

☐ Debating

☐ Mediating

☐ Telling stories

☐ Writing letters

☐ Thinking

☐ Requesting

☐ Setting an example

☐ Being a mate

☐ Taking criticism

☐ Taking risks

☐ Enjoying hobbies

☐ Budgeting

☐ Being a family member

Perfection was not required to check these items, since *nobody* does any of these perfectly or all of the time. However, if you checked a few of these and have managed to maintain reasonable sanity in a very complex world, give yourself a pat on the back. Remember, this was just a warm-up. The exercise that follows has been found to be very effective at building self-esteem.

Cognitive Rehearsal: An Exercise

1. Develop a list of ten positive statements about yourself that are meaningful and realistic and true. You may develop the statements from the list on the preceding pages, generate your own statements, or do both. Examples might include "I am a loyal, responsible member of my family (team, club, and so forth)"; "I am clean and orderly"; "I am a concerned listener." If you mention a role that you perform well, try to add specific personal characteristics that explain why. For example, instead of saying only that you are a good manager,

you might add that you size up situations quickly, react decisively, and treat people respectfully. Roles can change over time, but character and personality traits can be expressed across many different roles.

2. Write the ten positive statements in the space provided below.

3. Find a place to relax, undisturbed, for fifteen to twenty minutes. For one or two minutes, meditate on one statement and the evidence for its accuracy. Repeat this for each statement.

4. Repeat this exercise every day for ten days. Each day, add an additional statement in the space provided.

5. Several times each day, look at an item on the list and, for about two minutes, meditate on the evidence for its accuracy.

Ten Positive Statements

1.

2.

3.

4.

5.

6.

7.

8.

9.

10.

Additional Statements

1.

2.

3.

4.

5.

6.

7.

8.

9.

10.

If you prefer, you can write the statements on index cards and carry them with you. Some people find cards easier to refer to during the day.

Notice how you feel after practicing this skill, which disputes the all-or-nothing distortion of "I am no good" by substituting appreciative thoughts and feelings. I have found that people who try this exercise especially enjoy it. Read some of the comments they have said over the years.

- Hey! I am not so bad after all.

- I got better with practice. I didn't believe the statements at first. Then I found myself smiling on the way to school (or work).

- I feel *motivated* to act on them.

- I felt peaceful and calm.

- I learned that I have a lot more good than I give myself credit for.

CHAPTER 15

Cultivate Body Appreciation

The body is an external. It is not the core. One's body does not equal one's worth. However, the body is a metaphor for the core in that the way we experience the body is often similar to the way we experience our core selves.

The body, for example, is one way that we can receive and experience love. Consider the feeling of a hug or a gentle touch from someone who genuinely cares. The feeling that the body senses is also perceived by the inner core. If one views the body in the mirror with appreciation, it is easier to experience the core in a similar way. A respectful, caring attitude toward the body—reflected in sensible health practices—tends to positively influence one's feelings about the core self.

Conversely, through mistreatment or ridicule the body can be shamed and often, by extension, so is the core. If one thinks *I would appreciate my body if I didn't have that blemish or that wrinkle or that fat*, one would also be likely to place harsh conditions on loving the core self. If one is hard on one's physical imperfections, one will likely be unkind to the core self as well.

No matter how negatively one has come to view the body, however, or how negatively it has been treated, the inner core is still intact, responsive to healing, refreshing, and restorative love. As you cultivate appreciation for the body, it becomes easier to experience the core self more kindly. The exercise at the end of this chapter, then, will help you cultivate a wholesome appreciation for the body, no matter what its present condition may be. Although some in the world may have transmitted "X-rated," critical messages about your body, everyone can learn or relearn to experience the body positively.

The Magnificence of the Body

Dr. Russell M. Nelson (1988), who had a distinguished career as a heart surgeon, had great insight into the wonders of the body. He suggested that we consider the magnificent sights we have seen: a majestic mountain, a powerful horse gracefully galloping across a green meadow, a skyscraper. Then consider the magnificent body that you see in the mirror, he suggested, ignoring any imperfections for the moment. He noted that the word "magnificent" derives from two Latin roots: *magni* means "great," and *facere* means "to make." Thus, "magnificent," or "greatly made," well applies to the human body.

Let us begin to appreciate some of the wonders in the treasure chest that is the body.

From Conception to Maturity

At conception, a sperm and egg combine in a way that is only partially understood. From this union is formed a single cell that will multiply countless times according to a unique, unmatchable genetic code that is inherited—the sum of all of one's ancestors. The cells multiply according to this genetic code consisting of six billion steps of DNA. Though it could stretch the length of the adult's body, this genetic code is coiled within each cell's nucleus to a length of only 1/2,500 inch. Soon after conception, cells are producing over fifty thousand proteins needed for life. Although each cell contains the same genetic blueprint for the body and could turn into any kind of cell in the body, cells specialize by activating and repressing certain genes. Thus, some cells become cells of the eye, others become heart cells, and still others become needed blood vessels or nerves that appear in their proper places at the proper times. Over the course of a lifetime, the cells of the body will manufacture five tons of protein. Each day the mature body produces three hundred billion cells to maintain the body's total of seventy-five trillion cells. Placed end to end, the cells of the body would stretch 1,180,000 miles!

The Amazing Circulatory System

The heart brings life to every cell. Weighing only eleven ounces, this magnificent muscle tirelessly pumps two thousand gallons of blood each day, beating 2.5 billion times over the course of a lifetime—a pace that would tire other muscles in minutes. The heart actually is two pumps side-by-side. One propels blood forcefully enough that it circulates through the body's seventy-five thousand miles of blood vessels. The other sends blood to the lungs so gently that it does not damage the delicate air sacs there. When separated, cells of the heart beat with different rhythms. Together, however, they beat with the unison and synchrony of an exquisite symphony orchestra. Technology cannot replicate the heart's durability. The force of blood hurled against the aorta would quickly damage rigid metal pipes, while the flexible, tissue-thin valves of the heart are sturdier than any man-made materials.

The Sturdy Skeletal System

The 206 bones in the body are, ounce for ounce, stronger than solid steel or reinforced concrete. Unlike these man-made materials, bones become denser and stronger with weight lifting. Sixty-eight constantly lubricated joints allow for incredible continual movement. For example, the thirty-three vertebrae of the spine, supported by four hundred muscles and one thousand ligaments, permit an infinite variety of head and body positions. Or consider the vast capacities of the hand, which can powerfully turn the lid of a jar or delicately remove a splinter. For durability, precision, and complexity, science cannot duplicate the thumb, whose rotation requires thousands of messages from the brain. The hand will tirelessly extend and flex the joints of the fingers—twenty-five million times over a lifetime. With incredibly efficient utilization of space, the marrow of the bones will manufacture 2.5 million red blood cells each second, replenishing a supply of twenty-five trillion red blood cells, which, laid end to end, would reach thirty-one thousand miles into the sky.

Ponder also the role of the body's 650 muscles. A simple step takes two hundred muscles: forty leg muscles lift the leg, while muscles in the back maintain balance, and abdominal muscles keep you from falling backward.

Sensing the World

Sip a refreshing drink at a curbside cafe. You smell foods cooking and hear the sounds of people in animated conversation. You see multicolored flowers, see people strolling, see clouds lazily rolling, and feel the wind on your face. In less than a blink of an eye, complicated neural circuitry and countless signals in the brain allow you to sense the world around you. Let's consider the wonder of these capacities.

The eyes, ears, and nose are truly marvels of miniaturization. When you look at yourself in the mirror, you see in three dimensions though the image is entirely flat. Constant movement of the eyes, the equivalent to walking fifty miles a day, and tens of millions of receptors in the retina, which perform billions of calculations each second, make the eye more sensitive and priceless than any camera. Unlike a camera, the eyes are self-cleansing.

Conversation displaces the eardrum a distance equal to the diameter of a hydrogen atom. Yet the exquisitely sensitive ears enable us to distinguish individual voices and turn toward the source of the sound. In addition, the ears inform the brain of the slightest postural imbalance.

Compressed into an area smaller than a postage stamp, each nostril has ten million receptors for odors, enabling the brain to distinguish and remember up to ten thousand different scents.

Could you imagine a finer covering for the body than the skin? Under the average square centimeter (the size of the little finger's nail) are hundreds of nerve endings that detect touch, temperature, and pain. Not to mention one hundred sweat glands to cool and numerous melanocytes to protect from the sun's rays.

The Remarkable Defenses

Each moment, the body defends against an army of potent invaders with a defense system that is more sophisticated than any nation's. The skin forms the first line of protection. Its salty, acidic makeup kills many, many microbes and keeps many other impurities from entering the body.

Each day we inhale seventeen thousand pints of air, the equivalent of a small roomful of air, containing twenty billion foreign particles. The nose, airways, and lungs constitute a remarkable, self-contained air-conditioning and humidifying system. Lysozyme in the nose and throat destroys most bacteria and viruses. Mucus traps particles in the airways, and millions of tiny hairs, called cilia, vigorously sweep mucus back to the throat for swallowing. Powerful acid in the stomach neutralizes potent microbes, which is why a child can drink water from a puddle and usually remain healthy. In the nose, incoming air is conditioned to a constant 75 to 80 percent humidity. On cold days, additional blood is sent to the nose to warm the inhaled air.

Those microbes that evade destruction trigger a most remarkable flurry of activity. Billions of white cells relentlessly ingest or slay invaders that have entered the body. Other cells of the immune system multiply and summon antibody-producing cells. (A million different antibodies can be produced, each specific to a single microbe.) When needed, white cells can trigger fever that helps to defeat invaders and shut down fever when the battle is over. The lessons of the battle are preserved, as the immune system remembers the invader and the way to defend against it in the future.

Near the digestive tract, which absorbs needed nutrients, is the liver. In addition to five hundred other vital processes, this organ processes all nutrients absorbed by the intestines and neutralizes toxins. For example, in the eight seconds it takes for blood to flow through it, the liver greatly detoxifies caffeine or nicotine, which could be deadly if sent directly to the heart.

The Body's Wisdom

Overseeing the myriad complexities of the body is the brain. Weighing but three pounds and containing one hundred billion nerve cells, this organ makes even the finest computer seem crude by comparison. Since each nerve cell can connect with thousands of others, each in turn connecting to thousands of others, the flexibility, complexity, and potential of the brain is truly awe inspiring.

The brain, for example, keeps the interior of the body remarkably constant to preserve life. If a person is living in the desert in 120-degree weather, the brain directs more blood to the skin to release heat and increases perspiration. In the Arctic, blood is diverted from the skin to critical internal organs, while shivering generates heat. If a person bleeds, water is pulled from tissue into the blood vessels, and nonessential blood vessels constrict to keep blood pressure adequate. While maintaining internal equilibrium, the brain also makes decisions, solves problems, dreams, retrieves stored memories, recognizes faces, and affords unlimited capacity for wisdom and personality.

Other Wonders of the Body

Consider how the body converts the "grain of wheat once waving in a field" to "the energy expended by the wave of our hand" (National Geographic Society 1986) or to living tissue: first, by a complex series of transformations in the digestive tract, and then by even more complex transformations in the cells.

Appreciate for a moment the three hundred million alveoli, or air sacs, in the lungs, which exchange oxygen from the air we breathe for carbon dioxide from the body's cells. Spread flat, these alveoli would almost cover a tennis court.

Ponder the body's ability to repair itself. Unlike a table leg or a pipe, bones, blood vessels, skin, and other parts of the body can self-repair.

Many organs have a backup system: two eyes, two kidneys, two lungs. The single, vital liver, however, has an extraordinary capacity for regeneration. It will still function if 80 percent of it is destroyed or cut away, and, in just a few months, it can rebuild itself to its original size.

Contemplation of the complexities and magnificence of the body certainly helps us to regard our bodies with appreciation. Now let us turn to an exercise that also helps us experience our bodies with wholesome appreciation.

Body Appreciation: An Exercise

Do you see that the way you view your body influences the way you feel about your core self? Dwelling on the negative is a cognitive distortion that keeps your focus on negative thoughts at the expense of the positive. As a result, your mood can become generally negative. In a similar way, you can keep your focus on the most negative parts of your body. You might look in the mirror and focus on a blemish or a less attractive feature. Similarly, you might focus on fatigue, illness, or a part of the body that is not working well. (This is not to imply that you should ignore fatigue, illness, or pain. Rather, we're talking about the way you generally experience your body.) Soon, if you're not careful, you generally experience the body negatively.

To increase your body appreciation, do the following exercise for a minimum of four days.

At least six times throughout the day look at your body directly or in a mirror and notice, with appreciation, something that is *right* about it. Sometimes notice the jewels that were described above. Consider the miracles inside the body. Sometimes consider the skin, sensory organs, hands, fingers, or a feature that you consider attractive. Notice with appreciation what *is* working.

CHAPTER 16

Reinforce and Strengthen Body Appreciation

The exercise that follows was created by a well-known teacher of self-esteem, Jack Canfield (1985), and is a very effective way to reinforce the habit of experiencing the body with appreciation. The exercise takes about thirty minutes. Read it slowly, or have someone read it to you slowly, in a quiet place where you will be undisturbed. Complete this exercise once each day for four days.

A Body Appreciation Meditation

Welcome. Find a comfortable position, either sitting up in a chair or lying on your back on the floor or on a bed. Take a moment to get comfortable. And become aware of your body now. You may wish to stretch various parts of your body…your arms, your legs, your neck, or your back…just to heighten your awareness of your body. And now begin to take a few deeper, longer, and slower breaths…inhaling through your nose and exhaling through your mouth, if you are able to do that. And continue the long, slow, rhythmic breathing…

Now, let's take a few moments to focus on and appreciate your body. Feel the air flowing in and out of your lungs, bringing you life energy. Be aware that your lungs go on breathing, even when you are not aware of them…breathing in and out, all day long, all night long, even when you sleep…breathing in oxygen, breathing in fresh, pure air, breathing out the waste products, cleansing and restoring the entire body, a constant inflow and outflow of air…just like the ocean, like the tide coming in and going out. And so just now, send a beautiful and radiant white light and love to your lungs and realize that ever since you took your first breath your lungs have been there for you. No matter what we do, they still keep breathing in and out, all day long. Now become aware of your diaphragm, that muscle below your lungs that goes up and down and continually allows your lungs to breathe…and send light and love to your diaphragm.

Now become aware of your heart. Feel it and appreciate it. Your heart is a living miracle. It keeps beating ceaselessly, never asking for anything, a tireless muscle that continues to constantly serve you…sending life-giving nutrients throughout your body to every cell. What a beautiful and powerful instrument! Day in and day out your heart has been beating. And so see your heart surrounded by white light and warmth, and say silently, *I love you and I appreciate you*, to your heart.

Become aware now of your blood, which is pumped through your heart. It is the river of life for your body. Millions upon millions of blood cells…red corpuscles and white corpuscles… anticoagulants and antibodies…flowing through your bloodstream, fighting off disease, providing you with immunity and healing…bringing oxygen from your lungs to every cell in your body…all the way down to your toes and up into your hair. Feel that blood moving through your veins and arteries…and surround all of those veins and arteries with white light. See it dancing in the bloodstream as if it were bringing joy and love to each cell.

And now become aware of your chest and your rib cage. You can feel it rising and falling with your breathing…your rib cage that protects all of the organs in your body…protects your heart and your lungs…keeping them safe. So let yourself send love and light to those bones that make up your rib cage. And then become aware of your stomach and your intestines and your kidneys and your liver. All of the organs of your body that bring in food and digest it and provide the nutrients for your body…balancing and purifying your blood…your kidneys and your bladder. See your whole body from your neck down to your waist surrounded and filled with white light.

Next become aware of your legs…your legs that allow you to walk and to run and to dance and to jump. They allow you to stand up in the world, to move forward and to run and to make yourself breathless with exhilaration. Allow yourself to appreciate your legs and to feel them surrounded with white light. And see all the muscles and bones in your legs filled with radiant white light…and say to your legs, "I love you, legs, and I appreciate all the work that you've done." And then become aware of your feet. They let you stay balanced as you go through the world. They allow you to climb and to run…and they support you every day…and so thank your feet for being there and supporting you.

And then become aware of your arms. Your arms are miracles, too. And your hands. Think of all the things you are able to do because of your hands and your arms. You can write and type…you can reach out and touch things. You can pick things up and use them. You can bring food to your mouth. You can put things away that you don't want. You can scratch an itch, turn the pages of a book, cook food, drive your car, give someone a massage, tickle someone, defend yourself, or give someone a hug. You can reach out and make contact with your world and with others. So see your arms and your hands surrounded with light, and send them your love.

And then allow yourself to feel gratitude for having a body, one that you can use every day, to have the experiences you want to have, and that you need to grow and to learn from.

Then become aware of your spine, which allows you to stand up straight…and provides a structure for your whole body…and provides protection for your nerves that go from your brain down your spine and out to the rest of your body. See a golden light floating up your spine, from the base of your spine at your pelvis…floating up your spine one vertebra at a time, moving up your spine, all the way up to your neck…to the top of your spine where your skull connects…and let that golden light flow up into your brain.

And become aware of your vocal cords in your neck…they allow you to speak, to be heard, to communicate, to be understood, and to sing and to chant and to pray, and to shout, and yell with delight and excitement…to express your feelings and to cry and to share your deepest thoughts and your dreams.

Then become aware of the left side of your brain, the part of your brain that analyzes and computes, that solves problems and plans for the future, that calculates and reasons and deducts and inducts…just allow yourself to appreciate what your intellect provides for you… and see the left side of your brain totally filled with golden and white light…and shimmering little stars, and see that white light cleanse and awaken and love and nurture that part of your brain…and then let that light begin to flow across the bridge from the left side of your brain to the right side of your brain…the part of your brain that allows you to feel, to have emotions, to be intuitive, to dream…to daydream and to visualize, to create, and to talk to your higher wisdom…the part of your brain that allows you to write poetry and to draw…and to appreciate art and music. See that side of your brain filled with white and golden light.

Then sense that light flowing down the nerves into your eyes…and see and feel your eyes filled with that light, and realize the beauty that your eyes allow you to perceive: the flowers and the sunsets and the beautiful people…all the things that you've been able to appreciate through your eyes.

And then become aware of your nose. It allows you to smell and to breathe and to taste… all the wonderful tastes and smells in your life…the beautiful fragrances of flowers and the essence of all the foods that you love to eat.

Now become aware of your ears…they allow you to hear music, to listen to the wind, the sound of the surf at the ocean, and the singing of birds…and to listen to the words "I love you"…and to be in discussions and to listen to the ideas of another, to allow understanding to come forward.

And now feel every part of yourself from head to toe surrounded and filled with your own love and your own light. And now take a moment and allow yourself to apologize to your body for anything you may have done to it…for the times you weren't kind to it and for the times that you didn't care for it with love…the times that you didn't listen to it…for the times that you put too much food or alcohol or drugs into it…for the times you were too busy to eat, too busy to exercise…too busy for a massage or for a hot bath…and for all the times your body wanted to be hugged or touched and you held back.

And once again feel your body…and see yourself surrounded with light. And now let that light begin to expand out from your body…out into the world…expanding out, filling the space around you.

Now begin to bring that light slowly back into yourself, very slowly, back into your body, into yourself…and experience yourself here, now, full of light and full of love and appreciation for your body. And when you're ready, perhaps you begin to let yourself stretch and feel the awareness and aliveness back in your body. And when you're ready, you can slowly begin to sit up and readjust to being in the room and just let your eyes open, taking as much time as you need to make that transition.

Practice Increases Effect

This exercise can be quite powerful, and its effectiveness often increases with practice. As one relaxes and practices, useful feelings and insights may arise. Although the feelings that are experienced are usually quite pleasant, this may not always be the case. For example, one woman became tearful the first time she practiced this exercise, particularly when she tried to appreciate her legs. She had wanted, as a youth, to be a dancer, but her legs had been seriously burned in a fire. She realized that she still had anger about the accident and had hated her legs ever since. She determined to release the anger and the negative feelings she had for her body, and the next time she tried the exercise she was able to enjoy it greatly. So keep practicing, and expect the benefits to increase over time.

CHAPTER 17

Assert Self-Love and Appreciation

Let us return our attention directly to the core self and remember the premise that unconditional love is necessary for mental health and for growth. "Unconditional" means that we choose to love even though there are imperfections that we wish were otherwise.

Let's consider two people who are overweight. Jane thinks, *I am fat. I hate myself.* Mary thinks, *I am really glad inside to be me. I'd feel better and enjoy life even more if I lost some of this fat.* Notice the difference in emotional tones between Jane and Mary. Which one is more likely to adhere to an eating and exercise plan to lose weight? Which one is more likely to arrive at the desired weight without being emotionally distraught?

In chapter 6, "Acknowledge Reality—'Nevertheless!'" you learned the following key concepts:

1. A person can acknowledge unpleasant external conditions without condemning the core self.

2. People who dislike the self tend to use *because...therefore* thoughts (for example, *Because I am fat, therefore I hate myself*) that erode self-esteem.

3. The *nevertheless* skill provides a realistic, upbeat, immediate response to unpleasant externals—a response that reinforces one's sense of worth by separating worth from externals.

In this chapter, we adapt the *nevertheless* skill explored in chapter 6 to factor II, unconditional love, by using this format:

Even though _____, *nevertheless* _____:
(some external)   (some statement of love/appreciation)

For example: *Even though* I am overweight, *nevertheless* I love me.

Other *nevertheless* statements include:

- I sure love myself.

- Inside I am really glad to be me.

- Deep down, I really like and appreciate me.

Another variation is to use the *It's true* _____, *and* _____ format. For example, *It's true that I performed poorly today, and I love me.* Perhaps you can think of other sentences you like.

Even Though…Nevertheless: An Exercise

Select a partner. Ask your partner to say whatever negative statements come to mind, be they true or false, like:

I hate you!

You're a loser!

You're such a slob!

Why do you always screw up?

Put your ego on the shelf, and to each criticism respond with an *even though…nevertheless* statement that expresses love and appreciation for the core self. Again, you'll probably want to use some of your cognitive therapy or language of love skills (chapter 12). For example, if someone labels you "a loser," you can respond with, "Actually, I am a success who sometimes loses. *Even though* I sometimes lose, *nevertheless…*" If someone asserts that you always screw up, you can think to yourself, *Even though I sometimes screw up, nevertheless…*

Self-Love and Appreciation: An Exercise

1. For each of the next six days, select three events or situations with the potential to erode self-esteem (for example, you notice bags under your eyes when you look in the mirror; someone criticizes you or calls you a name; you perform poorly; you remember that someone you love doesn't love you).

2. In response to each event, select an *even though…nevertheless* statement that expresses love and appreciation. Then, on the following worksheet, describe the event or situation, the statement you used, and the effect that selecting this statement and saying it to yourself had on your feelings. Keeping a written record reinforces the skill.

3. This exercise allows you to experience challenging events with unconditional love. Such love is experienced as a *feeling*; try to say each statement with emotion. You might raise your chin a bit and place a pleasant expression on your face.

Remember that love is a feeling. It is also an attitude that wishes the best for you at each moment; and it is a decision that you make each day. Thus, intention and commitment are vital keys to loving yourself.

Date	Event/Situation	Statement Used	Effect
1. 2. 3.			
1. 2. 3.			
1. 2. 3.			
1. 2. 3.			
1. 2. 3.			
1. 2. 3.			

CHAPTER 18

Eyes of Love Meditation

The following exercise is a nice way to help you experience yourself joyfully and with appreciation.

First, find a quiet place to relax undisturbed, either lying or seated, for about ten minutes.

Once you have settled in, imagine that you are sitting in the presence of a very trusted and very loving being—a dear friend, a loving family member, God, or an imaginary being. This being sees you realistically and very lovingly. Imagine that you can see yourself through this being's eyes—the eyes of love. What is there to appreciate? Look thoroughly.

- Is there something pleasing or attractive physically?

- Notice all pleasing personality or character traits, such as intelligence, brightness, insightfulness, laughter, humor, integrity, peacefulness, good taste, or patience.

- Recognize all talents and skills.

- Note the appearance beyond pure physical attributes, such as your countenance, expression, or smile.

Behold yourself through the eyes of love and appreciation, and enjoy the experience for a few moments.

Now return to your own body. Feel all those feelings of love and appreciation from this loving being—and feel warm, happy, at ease, secure. Say to yourself silently, *I am lovable*, and feel those feelings of love and appreciation growing inside of you.

CHAPTER 19

Liking the Face in the Mirror

What are you worth?

Some people reply:

- I am worth $12.50 an hour. That's what my boss pays me.

- I am not worth anything. If you don't believe me, ask my dad (spouse, girlfriend, and so on).

- I'm worth only what I offer the morale of the troops.

As we discussed previously, we cannot put a finite value on the worth of an individual. Do we do it? Yes, if we reduce a person to salary, insurance policies, rank, position, talents, or what we can take from them. So let's repeat here the basic tenet of self-esteem: each person is of infinite, unchanging, and equal worth.

Have you ever taken a long time to look into your own eyes and see the core self? You can learn to like yourself in this way. It might take some practice, but this skill could change the way you think about mirrors.

The way other people view you may be distorted by the way they see themselves; however, a mirror reflects images quite accurately. When you view yourself in a mirror, your attention might be drawn to your appearance: clothes, hair, blemishes, or other externals. In the exercise that follows, however, you'll see yourself differently, perhaps differently than you ever have before. This is one of the most powerful exercises in this book. I am grateful to US Army Chaplain N. Alden Brown for teaching it.

A Reflection of Self: An Exercise

1. During the next four days, seek out a mirror several times throughout the course of each day.

2. Look into your eyes with the eyes of love. As you look, you might first notice that there is stress in and around the eyes. Look with real understanding and emotion. Try to understand what's behind the stress, and let it subside. As you look deeply with love you will notice a change in your eyes and in your entire countenance.

3. Repeat this exercise often. You can use any mirror, even a car mirror.

Over time, this simple yet profound exercise allows a very wholesome and good feeling to take root and grow. As you look into your eyes and see the core self, appearances and externals come to assume their correct (that is, secondary) level of importance. You might notice that you begin to look forward to and enjoy looking into the mirror instead of dreading it, because your focus is now on what is of infinite worth—the core—which you see with love.

CHAPTER 20

See Yourself Through Loving Eyes

Artistic expression can deeply affect us in ways that thinking may not. Developed by family therapist John Childers, this strategy uses art to experience unconditional love. The benefit of artistic expression lies in the process, not the quality of the art.

Step 1: Establish the Experience of Being an Artist

Within each of us is an artistic part of our personality. This artistic part is able to create new and wonderful drawings of the world around us. These drawings need not look exactly like a tree, house, or person. That is not important. What is important is the freedom to express your artistic self on paper. In a few minutes, as an artist, you'll create a wonderful drawing. But for now, just imagine being an artist.

Step 2: Identify Someone You Know Who Loves You

As an artist, you'll be drawing a picture of someone in your life who you know loves you (and has treated you respectfully). Take a moment to think about people in your life—perhaps a grandparent or other family member, a coworker, teacher, or dear friend. Select one very special person, a person you know loves you.

Step 3: Describe to Yourself the Characteristics That Make That Person Special

In a minute or two you'll draw a picture of this special person, but first think about how to draw this person. For example, how does this special person look? Is he or she tall, medium, or short in height? What color of hair does this special person have? What's the color of his or her eyes? Do the eyes sparkle? Does this person have a smiling face? Is this person reaching out with his or her arms? How does this person's voice sound? Does it sound soft? Loud? Strong? Kind? If voice sounds could be colors, what colors would this person's voice be? How would you describe this person's feelings? Continue to think about the qualities that make him or her special to you. As you think about this person who loves you, become aware of your own feelings. How are you feeling right now? Loving? Warm? Excited? Happy?

Step 4: Draw a Picture of the Person Who Loves You

Now let the artist within draw a picture of this special person—this person who loves you. Feel free to begin drawing now, selecting just the right crayons, pens, or pencils to color this person as you see him or her. You can use colors to describe this person's voice and feelings as well, or write a few words that describe him or her. Take your time and enjoy the process. As the artist, once you have completed your picture, you may want to give it a title.

Step 5: Imagine Being This Special Person and Being Able to See Yourself Through His or Her Loving Eyes

Now, I would like you to imagine that you are this special person you have drawn. Float outside of yourself and become this person who loves you. Now, as this special person, I would like you to think about how you see yourself. Look carefully.

Step 6: Describe and Draw What Is Loved and Seen Through Loving Eyes

Seeing yourself through the eyes of someone who loves you, you see yourself as someone to love. Describe to yourself what you love about the person you see. Continue seeing yourself through the eyes of someone who loves you. Now, please draw a picture of yourself as seen through these eyes. As you draw and color this picture, continue seeing yourself through loving eyes. Use colors and/or words to describe your looks, behaviors, and feelings. Your drawing may be lifelike or abstraction or splashes of color—whatever you choose to make it.

Step 7: Return Awareness to Your Own Body, Bringing Back Loving Feelings

Now, slowly come back into your own being. Looking at this picture of yourself, you see yourself as someone who is lovable. Seeing yourself as lovable, say silently to yourself, *I am lovable*, and notice the warm, loving feeling growing within you.

CHAPTER 21

Experience Love at the Heart Level

Thanks to recent advances in computer technology, we now know that filling the heart with love profoundly benefits both the mind and body. Throughout history, writers have described how emotions are experienced in the heart. Negative emotions might be experienced as "My heart is down," or "That broke my heart." Positive emotions might be described with phrases like "That touched my heart," "My heart is full of love," "I'm tender-hearted," "My heart took a picture," "heartwarming," or "heartfelt appreciation."

The Quick Coherence technique, described in this chapter, is a skill that helps us cultivate love at the heart level. A powerful complement to cognitive strategies, this skill first alters the heart, which in turn affects thinking and emotional well-being. The heart communicates to the brain and other parts of the body through neural, biochemical, biophysical (blood pressure), and electromagnetic messages. In fact, there is far more messaging from the heart to the brain than there is from the brain to the heart. This helps to explain why altering the heart can bring about so many beneficial changes in a person.

Your pulse rate reflects an average rate of beating of the heart (for example, seventy beats, per minute). The pulse rate is a fairly good indicator of one's physical and mental health, however, a better indicator is how well the heart adjusts its speed from beat to beat. *Heart coherence* means that the heart is adjusting speeds smoothly, flexibly, and quickly, as reflected in the left portion of the figure below. This pattern, which reflects balance within the nervous system, is associated with mental and physical well-being. Contrast this to the diagram on the right, which shows a more chaotic pattern associated with decreased health and well-being.

The description of heart coherence and the accompanying figure are adapted, and the Quick Coherence Technique® is reprinted, with permission, from D. Childre and D. Rozman (2003, 2005) and the HeartMath Institute, which has been researching emotional resilience for more than twenty-five years. For more about their research and resilience training, see heartmath.org.

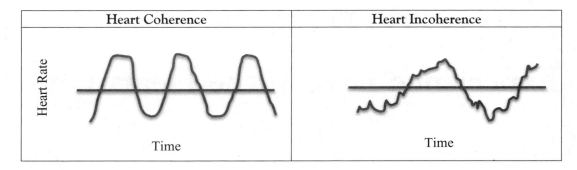

Heart coherence versus heart incoherence (adapted with permission from Childre and Rozman 2003, 21). The horizontal line represents average pulse rate, and the curved line represents beat-to-beat changes in heart rate.

Fortunately, people can usually achieve greater heart coherence within weeks to months by practicing the skill I will describe shortly. This skill uses positive emotions, particularly love, to change the heart. Ultimately, this skill helps us to more consistently respond to ourselves and others with greater love.

Preparations

Find a comfortable, relaxing place to prepare three written lists.

1. First, identify the person you love the most and write why you love that person. Take a moment to reflect on how that person makes you feel. Then make a list of your favorite people, in whose presence you perhaps feel or felt safe, secure, treasured, or appreciated. This list might include family, neighbors, teachers, friends, or even pets.

2. Make a list of experiences that made you feel loved and happy. You might recall moments when you felt embraced by nature, or moments with loving people.

3. Now make a list of moments when you felt caring, tenderness, respect, or compassion for someone. Perhaps a family member, or someone in need, comes to mind. Perhaps you remember holding a child and watching him or her sleep.

4. Pick one of these memories, one that is relatively free of negative emotions, to use in the Quick Coherence technique that follows. Experiencing any positive emotion—such as gratitude, appreciation, awe, peace, or contentment—elicits heart coherence. However, genuine, mature love is the quickest and most effective pathway to heart coherence, and it is most relevant to factor II of self-esteem. If you can, try to activate a feeling of love, and try to experience that feeling in the region of the heart when trying the Quick Coherence technique. If doing so is a stretch, pick another positive emotion at first, and then later try the skill using love. (If it is difficult to activate a positive emotion, you can even start by letting your heart go to neutral.)

The Quick Coherence Technique

This basic heart coherence technique only takes a minute, but it has powerful effects. Sit quietly and comfortably, focusing on your breath for a few moments to center yourself. Then follow these instructions (Childre and Rozman 2005, 44–45).

1. **Heart-Focused Breathing.** Focus your attention in the area of the heart. Imagine your breath is flowing in and out of your heart or chest area. Breathe a little slower and deeper than usual.

2. **Activate a Positive Feeling.** Make a sincere attempt to experience a regenerative feeling, such as appreciation or care for someone or something in your life.

Regarding step 2, remember that experiencing any positive emotion is beneficial at the heart level. However, mature love is the most effective pathway to heart coherence. So the goal of step 2 is to activate a feeling of mature love and to experience that feeling in the region of the heart. It is not so important in this exercise to remember details; what is important is to activate the feeling and to experience the feeling around the heart.

Practice this skill for at least four days, at least four times a day: upon wakening, before going to sleep at night, and two more times during the day. Initially, try it when you are calm. Later, you might try it when you need a break or to comfort yourself at stressful times of the day. Complete this record to track your experience.

Date	Event/Situation	Positive Emotion Activated	Effect
_____ 1. 2. 3. 4.			
_____ 1. 2. 3. 4.			
_____ 1. 2. 3. 4.			
_____ 1. 2. 3. 4.			

CHAPTER 22

Self-Compassion and Mindful Awareness

Being able to feel compassion for every human being, including yourself,
is a cornerstone of healthy self-esteem.

—Lisa M. Schab

We all suffer through difficult times. How do you typically act toward yourself when things go wrong? Take a moment to think about such times, which happen to everybody: you make a mistake; you fall short of a goal; you become aware of a personality shortcoming or a part of your body that bothers you; someone criticizes, scolds, teases, mistreats, or rejects you; you face setbacks that are not your fault; you get into a heated argument.

During such times, are you hard on yourself—self-critical—or kind? Which column below better describes how you typically act toward yourself during difficult times? Place a check next to each item that describes you.

Hard on Self (Self-Critical)	Kind to Self
☐ I use harsh, judgmental, disapproving, disrespectful language. (For example, "You idiot! Can't you do anything right?")	☐ I use self-caring, self-encouraging language. (For example, "This is difficult; keep trying.")
☐ I fixate on what's wrong with myself. ("I'm inadequate, a loser.")	☐ I remember what's right with myself.
☐ I'm intolerant of my weaknesses and anything short of perfection.	☐ I acknowledge flaws and weaknesses and accept myself.
☐ I see myself as a problem to be fixed and focus on fixing myself. I often feel shame and impatiently demand improvement. ("Do more, faster, better.")	☐ I'm patient and understanding with my imperfections; I focus on being happier and growing and improving.
☐ I ignore my suffering and pain.	☐ I acknowledge pain and pause to give myself comfort.
☐ I feel like I'm the only one going through this.	☐ I know that everyone suffers and struggles with feelings of inadequacy; lots of people feel as I do.
☐ I try to motivate myself with fear, anger, and punishment. (Perfectionism is driven by fear.)	☐ I motivate myself kindly.
☐ I'm hurt by my judgments of self and by others' judgments of me; I worry about impressions. ("What if I don't measure up?")	☐ I don't worry much about judgments. ("What's the big deal if people don't think well of me? It's not the end of the world if I try and fall short.")
☐ I blame myself.	☐ I try to understand how difficult things can be and then do my best.

Which style of relating to yourself feels better inside? Which better motivates you?

How Self-Critical Are You?

Now that you've taken a look at how you react during difficult times, please rate where you stand on the self-criticism scale below.

When things go wrong, are you typically:

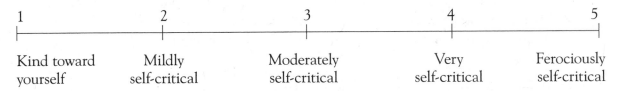

1	2	3	4	5
Kind toward yourself	Mildly self-critical	Moderately self-critical	Very self-critical	Ferociously self-critical

What Is Self-Compassion?

The kind way of relating to yourself is called "self-compassion," which has many benefits. Dr. Kristin Neff, the leading researcher on self-compassion, explains that compassion means to suffer with a person (2011). With self-compassion, then, we feel tender, warm feelings toward ourselves during difficult times. It is the Golden Rule in reverse—treating yourself as you would treat a good friend or loved one. If you feel self-compassion, then when the chips are down, you respond to your pain with understanding and kindness.

According to Neff (2011), self-compassion has three components:

1. **Mindful awareness of emotional distress** means we acknowledge and observe our thoughts, feelings, and bodily sensations in a calm, nonreactive, somewhat detached way. We simply notice what is going on inside at the moment, watching from a distance, as we might watch a cloud float across the sky. There are no judgments (good or bad) about what we experience; we simply accept whatever is being experienced at the moment.

   - We don't ignore or avoid our pain, because we must be aware of pain in order to heal or lessen it. Surprisingly, mindful awareness of our pain helps it to subside and helps us move beyond it.

   - When self-critical thoughts arise, as they often will, we simply note these with curious acceptance ("There's a critical thought—it's just a thought.") without getting carried away with them or buying into them.

   - Stepping back to watch the pain without being obsessed by it calms the mind and heart. More importantly, increasing mindful awareness, with its self-accepting stance, has been linked to improved self-esteem and happiness (Pepping, O'Donovan, and Davis 2013).

2. **Sense of common humanity** is the perspective that all of us are in the same boat: we all suffer. This perspective helps us feel less alone, less isolated. Everyone wants to be happy, to love and be loved, to succeed and grow, and to not suffer. Yet we all, at times,

feel inadequate and vulnerable, have shortcomings, make mistakes, and don't get what we want. This understanding helps us to not exaggerate our suffering, because we realize that others have suffered as much as we have. No one is being singled out. One is not different or better than another. Each person matters. Everyone's suffering matters.

3. **Being kind and supportive to yourself** means that you respond to your own pain inwardly—with kindness, warm understanding, patience, and deep caring—rather than with harsh criticism. Rather than self-condemnation, you offer yourself comfort, as you would a crying child, asking yourself, *How can I extend warmth, gentleness, encouragement, healing compassion?*

Self-compassion is closely related to unconditional love and empathy. "Empathy" is holding someone's pain in your heart with kind understanding. Empathy embraces the suffering person and says, "You are not alone. I'm here with you." Empathy listens without trying to talk someone out of his or her pain. Rather, empathy softens pain through its openhearted connection.

Self-compassion is not self-pity, avoiding responsibility to improve, or self-indulgence. In fact, people with self-compassion are more motivated to acknowledge weaknesses and persist in working toward constructive goals than those who don't have it. Like healthy self-esteem, self-compassion is linked to greater happiness and emotional well-being—and less depression, anxiety, and shame.

Believing that we are all in the same boat, self-compassionate people are less likely to think of themselves as superior or inferior to others. Understanding that all of us make mistakes and suffer as a result, self-compassionate people are more likely to forgive. They also tend to be kinder and less controlling of others.

Self-compassion quiets the harsh judgments that damage self-esteem. Importantly, self-compassion helps us regard all people, including ourselves, as worthwhile and worthy of care.

It is quite understandable if you have learned to be self-critical. Perhaps you internalized messages from harshly self-critical, abusive, or distant caregivers. Perhaps you never learned to be kind to yourself, to convey emotional warmth and soothing, healing messages. Instead you might have grown up hearing the following (adapted from Schab 2013, 19):

- You're not good enough.

- You're not trying…try harder.

- You'll never make it.

- What's wrong with you?

- You idiot! Loser!

- Can't you do anything right?

- Why can't you be like your sister?

- You're worthless.

- I don't love you.

- You're bad.

- Why are you so lazy?

Self-criticism can become habitual. We might think it protects against the negative judgments of self and others, that it keeps us in line and stops us from making mistakes. As Neff (2011) explains, self-criticism can provide a false sense of superiority ("At least I'm smart enough to see how inadequate I am and fair enough to punish myself for my mistakes."). It can also feed false pride ("I'm so used to excellence that it's beneath me to fail."). We might even find that self-criticism affords a kind of protection ("I'll beat my critical parent to the punch, and thus gain his approval.").

In the long run, however, self-criticism is exhausting and depressing. Self-criticism is an emotional attack on the self. Just like a physical attack, self-criticism activates the stress response, which over time dampens pleasure and depletes energy.

Beating oneself up saps motivation and self-confidence. The distressing emotions linked to self-criticism create urges to act in self-destructive ways. Neff (2011) explains that fear creates urges to escape and avoid our problems. Anger creates the urge to attack, to take out our pain on others, and to be critical of others. Shame creates the urge to hide from people, cover flaws, and seek quick fixes to our problems. In contrast, self-compassion nourishes self-acceptance and the urge to grow.

In short, self-compassion is a much more effective motivator than self-criticism—a more effective pathway to psychological health, inner peace, and growth. Fortunately, through practice we can learn to replace self-criticism with self-compassion.

- Rather than trying to suppress or ignore pain, which actually *increases* the time we spend thinking about it, we learn to give pain full, kind attention. We acknowledge that the pain exists and that it is valid and important.

- Rather than constantly bracing and battling against the pain, we instead *embrace* it. Curiously, changing our response to pain in this way typically eases the pain. It is like holding and soothing a crying child. Eventually, the crying stops and the child returns to playing.

You might think of self-compassion as bringing unconditional love to your own suffering, which is what the following exercise and the next three chapters will help you to do.

Practicing Mindful Awareness: An Exercise

We'll start growing self-compassion by increasing the capacity to mindfully observe. This exercise, developed by Dr. Christopher Pepping, has been found to improve self-esteem (reprinted with permission from Pepping, Davis, and O'Donovan 2016). Find a comfortable, quiet place to sit where you will not be disturbed for fifteen minutes. Follow the instructions by either reading the script or recording it and then listening to it.

I am now going to take you through a fifteen-minute guided mindfulness meditation. The purpose of this meditation is not necessarily to feel more relaxed or calm or better than you did at the start of the meditation. The purpose is to just simply practice mindfulness. Take a few moments now to settle into a comfortable position—wiggle into a position that makes your back straight, but not rigid. Place your feet squarely on the ground. If you wear glasses, you may want to take them off. Gently close your eyes if you feel comfortable doing so. And if not, just find a spot on the floor to focus on.

Feeling all the points of contact between your body and the chair, and just settling into the stillness. Let's begin by just noticing that you can feel your feet on the ground. Notice that you can feel the bottom of your feet in your shoes. Just settling into this…bringing attention now to the feeling of the palms of your hands. And either paying attention to what you're touching or the feeling of contact. Or perhaps the feeling of the air or the temperature of the air on your palms. And just bringing all your attention and awareness to this part of the body.

And now shifting attention to the sensation of breathing. We're not trying to change the breath in any way. It doesn't have to become deeper or slower or calmer. Just paying attention to the breath as it is in this moment. Throughout this meditation we will be using the breath as an anchor. So every time you find that your mind wanders, and you start thinking or responding to sounds or thoughts as they arise, every time you notice this, just time and time again bring your mind back to the breath—that is, bring your attention back to the breath. And so now, for the next few moments, just sitting and bringing your attention to the feeling of the in-breath, and the feeling of the out-breath. Holding in awareness that part of the body where the breath feels most vivid or strong for you. It might be your abdomen, or your chest or nose or throat. Just bringing all your attention and awareness to that part.

Every time you find your mind has wandered, just gently bring your attention back to the breath. You may already find that your mind has wandered. And your mind is just doing what minds do. You may be noticing thoughts about the meditation, whether you are doing it right, whether this is boring. You may have thoughts about how relaxing or calming this feels. No matter what your thoughts are, just know that they are thoughts; they're mental events that come into the mind, and just as easily, if you leave them alone, they will also go out of your mind, and they will be replaced by more thoughts. You may be noticing bizarre or random thoughts. You might be planning what you will do for the rest of the day, or tomorrow.

The purpose of a mindfulness meditation is not to stop your thoughts or suppress them or resist them or get rid of them. It's just to know that you're thinking, and then to shift your attention back to the breath. So your thoughts become like background chatter—like a radio going in the background. They are there, your mind is chattering away, and you are just not getting caught up in it.

Just noticing your breathing and what is happening in the present moment.

So just bringing your attention to where the mind is now. And if you need to come back to the breath, then gently bring your mind back. You may also like to notice the reactions, when you find that your mind has wandered when you bring awareness to the focus of the thoughts. Perhaps you have a reaction that you don't want to be having this thought, or you shouldn't be having this thought at the moment. Perhaps, if you are finding it difficult for your mind to settle, your reaction is that it shouldn't be this way, or that this is hard. Just notice those thoughts as thoughts. Your mind giving a commentary of what it is thinking at the moment. Nothing more and nothing less. The thoughts are not necessarily true. The thoughts are not necessarily things to be believed. And the thoughts are not necessarily things to be acted upon. Just let the thoughts do their thing, and just bring your attention back to the breath, no matter what your thoughts are telling you.

So breathing in, and breathing out…just simply observing the breath, in this moment. And now in this moment. Just breathing in, and just breathing out. Being aware of everything that is happening, in each moment, as it passes. Your thoughts are going to be there whether you want them to be there or not. So you may as well just let them. But bringing your attention to the experience of breathing in, and breathing out. And letting your thoughts come and go as they will. And you may be noticing themes to your thoughts—these are the "hard" and "boring" thoughts. These are the "planning" thoughts. Perhaps these are self-critical thoughts or worries about measuring up. Just when you notice the theme of the thoughts, just remember they are just thoughts, too, and bring your attention back to the breathing.

You may be also becoming aware of feelings and sensations from sitting for this amount of time. You may be noticing themes of discomfort, or itches as you sit. See if you can experience these just as sensations. You may notice thoughts like *This really hurts*, or *This is unbearable*, or *I have to scratch*. And again, just because they're thoughts doesn't mean they are real or that you have to obey them. Just be willing to experience the thoughts and sensations—be open to allowing them to be there. Holding the thoughts or sensations in one part of awareness, and focusing on the breath at the same time.

And observing your mind's reaction. Perhaps your mind is irritated. Perhaps your mind is telling you to scratch, or to move. And if you do decide to move, or to scratch, just do so mindfully. And then just coming back to the breath, and allowing things to be, just as they are. Just breathing in, and just breathing out. Letting thoughts and sensations just enter awareness and then leave awareness. And continue to focus on your breath. Mindfulness is awareness of everything that is happening in the present moment. Just allowing awareness to be there. Being willing to have the experience you are having. And just breathing in, and just breathing out.

Being aware of whatever is happening in the present moment. If you find you're lost in thoughts, just notice where your mind went. And bring your mind back to the breath. You might find that the background chatter becomes less noticeable. Or maybe it doesn't. Regardless of what's happening…just come back to the breath.

And now bring your attention and awareness to the feeling in your body on the chair and all the points of contact between you and the surface. And now just notice that you can feel your feet on the ground. Notice that you can feel the bottom of your feet in your shoes.

Then bring your attention to the palms of your hands. Whether they are touching the chair or your body, or whether you can just feel the temperature of the air on them…just bringing your attention to the palms of your hands. Now gently bring your attention and awareness of the room around you. And when you're ready, open your eyes, and come back to the room.

Before rushing off to go about your day, take a moment to notice how you now feel. How does your body feel? Your mind? Often people notice that they feel more settled, more at peace—that simply accepting what is, without struggling, resisting, trying to change things, or judging, is restful. Whether what you notice is or is not restful, just notice it with curious, nonjudgmental interest. This is the essence of mindful awareness.

Practice this exercise at least once a day for the next four days. Try to simply sit with whatever you notice in a kind, curious, nonjudgmental way. Whatever you think, feel, or sense is okay. Be present with whatever arises without reacting to it. Simply respond to it with kind acceptance.

CHAPTER 23

Meet Pain with Self-Compassion

The curious paradox is that when I accept myself just as I am, then I can change.

—Carl Rogers

Compassion is sometimes called gentle friendliness, loving-kindness, deep caring, genuine concern, or empathy. This chapter helps cultivate compassion, first for others, and then for yourself.

Try these exercises, adapted from Schab (2013, 133–137).

Planting the Seeds of Compassion: An Activity

Record the level of concern or empathy you would feel for each of the following people or animals on a scale of 1 (low) to 10 (high). Then write the feeling or feelings that best describe your reaction to the situations. Write your own, or choose from the following list:

Pain	Helplessness
Sadness	Anger

1. Your friend whose parent has died

Concern/empathy: _____ Feeling(s): _____

2. Your best friend is dying

Concern/empathy: _____ Feeling(s): _____

3. A puppy limping in the street in the rain

Concern/empathy: _____ Feeling(s): _____

4. A person on the news who lost everything in a hurricane

Concern/empathy: _____ Feeling(s): _____

5. A child who has a terminal illness

Concern/empathy: _____ Feeling(s): _____

6. A disabled child who is walking with crutches

Concern/empathy: _____ Feeling(s): _____

7. Your parent or grandparent who is aging

Concern/empathy: _____ Feeling(s): _____

8. A loved one who was harshly criticized by another family member

Concern/empathy: _____ Feeling(s): _____

9. A blind kitten

Concern/empathy: _____ Feeling(s): _____

10. A homeless person on the street

Concern/empathy: _____ Feeling(s): _____

11. Someone on the side of the highway whose car has broken down

Concern/empathy: _____ Feeling(s): _____

12. A friend who lost a child in a car accident

Concern/empathy: _____ Feeling(s): _____

13. A family who lost a child to suicide

Concern/empathy: _____ Feeling(s): _____

Check any of the following statements you might use when you are speaking with compassion.

☐ "I'm sorry this happened to you."

☐ "How can I help?"

☐ "Are you okay?"

☐ "Tell me what I can do."

☐ "I want to help."

☐ "It will be okay."

☐ "I will help you through this."

☐ "I care about you."

☐ "It will get better."

☐ "I'm glad you told me about this."

☐ Other: _____

Circle any of these compassionate actions you are comfortable doing.

Listening	Hugging
Giving energy	Paying attention
Giving time	Giving emotional support
Giving financial support	Affectionately patting someone's shoulder or arm

Other: _____

Choose two of the above situations (1–13) and describe how you would treat that person or animal with compassion.

Number _____

What I would say: _____

What I would do: _____

Number _____

What I would say: _____

What I would do: _____

Now Try This

What are your thoughts and feelings about treating yourself with compassion?

_____

_____

_____

    You may not be used to directing compassion toward yourself, but if you know how to treat others with compassion, you also know how to treat yourself. Think about the compassionate words and actions listed above, and describe how you could show compassion for yourself in the following situations.

You've had a rough day.

Compassionate words: _____

Compassionate actions: _____

You disappoint your boss.

Compassionate words: _____

Compassionate actions: _____

You disappoint yourself.

Compassionate words: _____

Compassionate actions: _____

Someone gets angry with you for something you did.

Compassionate words: _____

Compassionate actions: _____

You made a big mistake.

Compassionate words: _____

Compassionate actions: _____

Someone criticized you.

Compassionate words: _____

Compassionate actions: _____

The following skill is adapted, with permission, from Dr. Kristin Neff's excellent website, http://www.self-compassion.org. It is a very effective skill for when you feel emotional pain—suffering in any difficult circumstance. When you are upset, sad, self-critical, or hurt, try it. (First try this skill when you are not too distressed; as you gain comfort with it, you can use it for more distressing times.)

The Basic Self-Compassion Meditation

Allow yourself to really get in touch with all the difficult feelings and sensations. Remember the phrase, "Whatever I feel is okay. Let me feel it." Place both hands gently over your heart. Feel the warmth in your hands, the rhythmic rise and fall of your chest. Perhaps rub or soothe your heart area. Breathe in compassion on the in-breath, imagining soothing affection and kindness for yourself. Repeat these four statements either silently or aloud, softly, with kind acceptance. Notice that the first is a statement of mindful awareness, the second of shared humanity, and the last two of kindness.

1. This is a moment of suffering

2. Suffering is a part of life.

3. May I be kind to myself in this moment.

4. May I give myself the compassion I need.

With each breath, feel kind understanding filling your heart and soothing your body.

When you have finished repeating the four phrases several times, notice if the present moment is somewhat less difficult than a moment ago.

Memorize the four statements, and use them in any difficult moment. If you prefer, you might experiment with other statements, such as the ones in the table below.

Mindful Awareness	Shared Humanity	Kindness
This is difficult. This is really hard right now. It hurts to feel this now. Yes, there is pain. This is a struggle for me. This is rough, and I'm in need of care.	We all suffer. Suffering is part of being human. Every person suffers. It is normal to feel this way. Many others have experienced what I'm going through.	May I hold this pain with caring. May I be as kind as possible. May I be understanding. I'm so sorry you're in pain. This suffering is worthy of compassion and comfort. "Soften, soothe, allow."* "I'm a worthwhile human being who is suffering."* "May I be gentle and understanding with myself."*

* From Neff 2011, 114, 49, 119, respectively.

Difficult Moments: An Activity

Write down four statements that you will use throughout the day: one for mindful awareness, one for shared humanity, and two for meeting your pain with kindness. Memorize these. Then use them for three difficult moments throughout the day for four consecutive days. Keep a log relating to how your practice affects your thoughts, feelings, and bodily sensations.

Statement 1. (mindful awareness): _____.

Statement 2. (shared humanity): _____.

Statement 3. (kindness): _____.

Statement 4. (kindness): _____.

Day	Difficult Moment	Effect on Thoughts, Feelings, and Bodily Sensations
Day 1 1. 2. 3.		
Day 2 1. 2. 3.		
Day 3 1. 2. 3.		
Day 4 1. 2. 3.		

CHAPTER 24

Experience Self-Compassion at the Body Level

Have you ever noticed where you experience negative emotions? Usually people say that it is in their bodies, not their heads. Changing our negative thinking can often soften negative emotions. However, many people find that soothing the body can be even more effective than trying to fight negative thoughts. We have learned that trying to suppress, avoid, or get rid of negative thoughts and feelings actually increases awareness of them. The approach that we'll explore in this chapter *acknowledges* pain, changing only the way we *respond* to the pain. The new response is nonjudgmental self-compassion at the body level.

Self-Compassion and Loving-Kindness

The soften, soothe, allow meditation takes about fifteen minutes.

1. Sit comfortably in a quiet place or go on a solitary walk.

2. Pause to notice your breathing, noticing all the sensations as you breathe in and as you breathe out, such as the rising and falling of the chest, and air flowing in and out. Rest in your breath, letting your mind clear, enjoying a moment of restful, peaceful quiet.

3. Select a difficult time that hurt your self-esteem or caused painful emotions, such as shame, hurt, worry, aloneness, guilt, fear, or rejection.

This chapter is adapted, with permission, from Dr. Kristin Neff's website, http://www.self-compassion.org. The Soften, Soothe, Allow Meditation is from the Mindful Self-Compassion Program, http:// www.CenterforMSC. org, and was codeveloped with Dr. Chris Germer. The loving-kindness intentions at step 12 are from the Self-Compassion/Loving-Kindness Meditation.

4. Remembering the suffering, be aware of the source of the suffering and the resulting feelings. Perhaps you feel frightened, disappointed, inadequate, worthless, angry, or isolated. Simply notice and name the feelings, without getting too involved in the story line. Notice the feelings without judging them as good or bad. Whatever you feel is okay.

5. Which is the most uncomfortable emotion now? With gentle acceptance and without resisting, notice where in your body you sense that most uncomfortable emotion. Perhaps you feel tightness in your head, shoulders, or throat; tension in the forehead or eyes; heaviness in your heart; the stomach turning over; or numbness. Then see if you can describe to yourself the sensation, such as "numb," "tight," "cold," "hot," or "tingling."

6. With caring curiosity, notice if the hurt increases with harsh self-criticism, beating yourself up for not measuring up, or demanding perfection. Just notice without judging. Greet even harsh criticism with kind awareness. You might even thank your harsh inner critic for trying to help you. Allow the area that holds the discomfort to soften. Just sit quietly and calmly with the discomfort.

7. Place your hand gently over that spot in a soothing, comforting, warm way. Maybe gently patting, caressing, or rubbing that area in a small, reassuring circle—any way that confers caring, tenderness, love, or comfort. If you can't physically touch yourself, you can imagine a soothing touch to that area. Or try a warm hug or squeeze. Just allow that discomfort to be there. Don't fight it or force it away. You are safe now.

8. Let your face express a soft, gentle, loving half-smile. Think of a parent affectionately gazing at a sleeping child as you look at your pain.

9. Breathe in soothing compassion to that area of the body with each in-breath. With each out-breath, release tension.

10. Whenever you find yourself thinking—your mind wandering, judging, worrying, or criticizing—gently escort attention back to that part of the body, breathing into and out from that area of the body. As you do, repeat the phrase "soften, soothe, allow." Notice what shifts as you do. Perhaps tension eases, dissipates, or breaks up. Whatever occurs, or does not occur, just stay with that with curious interest.

11. Now let awareness of the area that holds the pain dissolve, as you move awareness to your entire body—your breathing, your movements, all sensations, your feelings of caring for what you are going through. Remembering that we are all imperfect, remembering that life is imperfect. If we are open to all of this, we can be happy even in the face of suffering.

12. To end, reinforce the intention to be compassionate. Place your hands over your heart as you repeat the following:

- May I be safe.

- May I be peaceful.

- May I be kind to myself.

- May I accept myself as I am.

As you keep repeating these phrases, offer yourself kindness and compassion, the same way you would offer kind support to a good friend who is feeling bad. Notice the hands over your heart. Take some deeper breaths. Get in touch with how it feels to experience compassion…perhaps warm, openhearted, courageous, peaceful, or authentic. Good feelings are also part of the human experience. Remember that everyone is in the same boat. Savor the experience of directing goodwill toward yourself. If your mind wanders, just refresh the phrases in your mind.

13. When you are ready, thank yourself for being a good, supportive friend. Stretch and then get on with your day.

This meditation can be a very effective way to cope with difficult times without overthinking or getting swept away by drama. The phrases at step twelve are loving-kindness intentions. Practicing such phrases has been shown to confer a wide range of emotional and physical benefits, including increased self-compassion (Davidson 2007), self-acceptance and positive emotions (Fredrickson et al. 2008), and reduced self-criticism (Shahar et al. 2015).

Practice the meditation at least once a day for four days. Complete this record to track your progress.

Date	Time of Day	Effects on Body	Effects on Emotions
1.			
2.			
3.			
4.			

Note: Research (Hutcherson, Seppala, and Gross 2008) has shown that the practice of directing loving-kindness intentions toward others increases positive feelings about others. To increase compassion for others, repeat this meditation, reciting "May you be safe. May you be peaceful. May you be kind to yourself. May you accept yourself as you are."

CHAPTER 25

Compassionate Journaling

Our own wounds can be vehicles for exploring our essential nature, revealing the deepest textures of our heart and soul, if only we will sit with them, open ourselves to the pain…without holding back, without blame.

—Wayne Muller

As we discussed in chapter 22, everyone suffers. Most people carry painful childhood and adult memories. Dr. James Pennebaker, a psychology professor at the University of Texas at Austin, has led the research in journaling about difficult times and emotional upheaval, including trauma. He reasons that ignoring or holding in strong negative emotions is not healthy, and that writing about difficult times is beneficial. Pennebaker has asked many groups of people—Holocaust survivors; combat veterans; people whose spouses committed suicide or died in car accidents; survivors of natural disasters, divorce, abuse, or job firings; "normal" college students; and others—to write about their most difficult experiences. Typically, they write for twenty minutes each day for four days, expressing their deepest thoughts and feelings about their experiences.

Since the 1980s more than three hundred studies have lent support to Pennebaker's reasoning. Physically, those who journal experience better sleep, less pain, and fewer illnesses. Psychologically, they show improved well-being and happiness and less depression, anxiety, anger, shame, and worry. Journaling even improves thinking ability and work efficiency.

This chapter summarizes the work of Dr. James W. Pennebaker (1997) and Pennebaker and John F. Evans (2014). The guidelines and instructions for confiding in writing, and the summary of supporting research, are adapted with permission.

Why Is Journaling Beneficial?

Trying *not* to think about painful memories consumes enormous amounts of energy and leaves the pain unchanged. Paradoxically, giving respectful attention to our pain helps to soothe and lessen the pain so that we can better move beyond it.

Writing in a safe, paced way slows things down. It enables us to get in touch with and honor all parts of ourselves—who we are—even in difficult times. It helps us better understand ourselves and our difficulties. It allows us to bring healing compassion to psychological wounds and to restore a sense of wholeness.

As you honor your pain, you'll more clearly see that there is self-worth both in and beyond your pain. As you face, rather than avoid, the pain, you'll likely discover a few things.

- A sense of relief from releasing long-held secrets

- Strengths that got you through the difficult time, and perhaps protected you or others from further harm

- Resilience, and confidence that you can cope in the present because you got through your most difficult times

- Different ways to interpret the event and accept it with more peace

- Opportunities to respond to yourself with compassion rather than harsh judgments and self-criticism

- Opportunities to reaffirm your worth, your belief in your authentic self, and your hope for the future

- Gratitude for what's left (for example, friends, abilities, senses, food, education, opportunities, and beauty)

- Ways to redirect your attention to more positive aspects of life

- Ways to grow and bring new meaning to your life

Who Benefits from Journaling?

Nearly everyone benefits from journaling, irrespective of one's gender or country of residence, because keeping secrets about traumas seems to be particularly predictive of medical and psychological problems. Males and people who are angry or out of touch with their emotions especially benefit.

Journaling is useful for all traumas and adversities, especially if the event was unexpected, unwanted, and hard to talk about. If you are still troubled by the past, think about it often, and expend significant energy trying to avoid thinking about it, it may be useful to try journaling. The greatest benefits seem to occur for those who wanted to confide in others but had never done so.

Guidelines and Considerations

- It's good to establish a writing ritual: write at the same time each day, and allow time to reflect afterward. Ideal times might be on weekends, during vacations, or at the end of the day. Write in a comfortable, secure, private environment, such as a private room, library, coffee shop, or park. It's better to write when conditions are less than ideal than to not write at all. Use a notebook, journal, sheets of paper—whatever you prefer.

- Don't write until you feel ready. Before writing about a traumatic event, it is probably best to wait several weeks after its occurrence to allow things to settle down emotionally.

- Understandably, when writing about painful experiences, you might experience a short slip in mood. You might feel sad or even depressed—particularly in the first day or two. This is normal. These feelings usually last a few minutes, or occasionally hours, and rarely a day or two. You might feel much like you do after seeing a sad movie. Some people cry as they write, or dream about past events. Afterward, however, most people feel relief and contentment for up to six months. They typically report that they better understand the past and that it no longer hurts to think about it.

- If you feel that writing might cause you to fall over the edge, then ease up, write about another topic, or simply stop writing. If writing for at least four days doesn't make you feel better, consider seeking the help of a mental health professional specializing in trauma (see the "Recommended Resources" section to locate a trauma specialist). Pennebaker notes that among his thousands of research subjects, no one has lost control. Only three saw a psychologist, and all three wanted to continue with the writing study they were involved with.

- After each journal session, notice the degree to which you expressed your deepest thoughts and feelings, and pay attention to how you now feel. Think about how valuable the day's writing has been. Over the course of the four days, notice if anything has shifted or changed with regard to your mood or understanding.

The four-day writing exercise below has been the most rigorously tested. Try it for four days, without reading ahead. Then you might try the additional journal approaches that follow.

Basic Four-Day Journaling: An Exercise

1. Find a quiet place where you won't be interrupted for at least twenty minutes. A neutral place, such as a table placed in the corner of a room, works well.

2. Write continuously for about twenty minutes about what troubles you most—what keeps you awake at night, what you dwell on, what you try to avoid. Ideally, it should be about something you have not talked about with others in detail. Don't worry about grammar, spelling, or punctuation.

3. Clearly describe the event. What was going on before? What happened during and after? Who were the main characters? What where they doing, feeling, and thinking? What were you doing, thinking, and feeling? How has the experience affected you? How has it affected others? *Discuss your deepest thoughts and especially your deepest feelings about the experience.* Make your writing personal and heartfelt, not distant or intellectual. Name and accept all feelings. (Remind yourself, "Whatever I feel is okay.") You might explore how this event is related to your childhood; your relationships with family members, friends, lovers, and others of importance; your work; and your place in life. You might link the event to who you have been in the past, are now, and would like to become. Has the event changed the way others view you? How you view yourself? It is okay to start with glaring holes. Over the course of the four days, many of these aspects are likely to become clearer.

4. You can write about the same event for all four days. Many find that understanding deepens, and a sense of closure occurs over the course of the four days. However, it's okay if you find yourself moving to another topic. Trauma can spill over and affect other areas of life, such as marriage issues. Trust where your writing takes you, as long as the topics are emotionally important. If you find yourself writing about trivial distractions, return to the difficult event. If you get bored with writing about the difficult event, and the painful experience seems settled, switch to another troubling topic. Consider any topic you've been avoiding.

5. Write for your eyes only. If you worry about someone reading it, you may not write what you honestly feel. Hide or destroy your writing if you fear someone might see it.

6. If you can, try writing on four consecutive days. It's okay to skip days, but the sooner you complete the writing exercise, the better. If necessary, you might fit in writing in another way that works better for you (for example, once a week for four weeks).

7. Write for at least twenty minutes for four days. You can write for additional days if you find that writing opens up other issues to think about.

8. If you write every day and find that you are writing about the same topic with little change in words or little relief, perhaps it's time to take a break from writing, or at least a break from this topic.

9. If a topic makes you overly distraught, ease up. Approach it gradually, try a different topic, or stop writing.

10. You can try this before bed if you associate insomnia with intrusive memories at bedtime. Journaling is a useful way to accept the worries, rather than fight them, and to clean out the mind.

11. Take out your journal at any future time you feel the need, for as long or short of a time that you feel is best. Studies have found benefits from writing for just a few minutes to up to thirty minutes.

After the Four-Day Journaling Exercise

Additional benefits might come from completing additional journaling exercises, perhaps trying different approaches. After completing the four-day journaling exercise, give yourself at least two or three days before reviewing what you wrote. Consider the following:

- Over the course of the four days, did you find it easier to let go and open up, expressing your deepest thoughts and feelings? Did you feel a sense of closure and greater understanding after the four days? Would additional writing help?

- Over the course of the four days, did you repeat what you had written, suggesting that processing is stuck? Or did you open up to different aspects or perspectives? How might the following help to broaden your perspective in beneficial ways?

  - Did you acknowledge both bad and good outcomes, which increases the benefit of writing? What have you lost, and what have you gained as a result of this upheaval?

  - Did your writing contain both negative and positive emotions? It is helpful to acknowledge negative feelings without dwelling in self-pity or beating yourself up. However, adding positive emotions increases the benefits of journaling. Did your writing include positive words like "love," "caring," "courage," "funny," "warmth," "dignity," "accepting," "calm," or "meaning"? You might try replacing negative emotions like "sad," "uptight," "worried," or "dispirited" with more positive phrases, like "not happy," "not calm," or "knocked off my usual positive course."

  - It helps to use insight words like "cause," "effect," "because," "reason," "rationale," "understand," "realize," "know," and "meaning." Such words suggest active attempts to understand one's story better, make sense of the experience, and construct meaning.

Notice that expanding your perspective is not phony positive thinking that minimizes pain or trauma. (Statements like "Keep a stiff upper lip" or "You'll laugh at this someday" are not helpful.) Rather, it is about actively looking for actual benefits, such as greater understanding, a kinder perspective, wisdom, or constructive change in your life's direction. Perhaps the subject of seeking or offering forgiveness comes up (see chapter 31).

If you are stuck, try to step back and write about the event from a different perspective. Here are some possibilities.

- Change to third person when writing about yourself (for example, "He felt...").

- Indicate what you'd like others to know.

- Personal singular pronouns (I, me, mine) suggest self-focus, which is good. However, try writing about other people and their perspectives.

- Write a compassionate letter to a best friend, whom you imagine suffered a similar experience. What might that friend have been going through at the time? What advice, encouragement, or other expressions of kindness, concern, or understanding would you give? What might your friend learn about himself or life? How might your friend grow?

- Write a letter from a real or imaginary compassionate friend to yourself (Neff 2011). This friend knows you—your strengths, weaknesses, and the challenges you've faced—and is unconditionally loving and accepting. Your friend understands that humans are imperfect and also knows that you are much more than your failings. What would that friend tell you? How would that friend convey affection and support (for example, "I care about you"; "I want you to be whole and happy"; "You are only human")? Perhaps that friend knows you well enough to say, "You sound like your critical father. It must be so hard to be so harshly critical, when all you really want is to be accepted and loved so you can be your best. I know you are just trying to keep yourself in line and to improve. Wouldn't kindness and encouragement work better than harsh self-criticism?" If you need to make changes in your life, how might that compassionate friend respectfully suggest these changes? Notice how your body feels as you write this compassionate letter, and let feelings of compassion sink in. Put the letter aside when you are finished. Come back after a day or two to reread the letter and let the feelings of compassion sink in further.

- In addition to honoring your suffering, you might ask, "Is there something about the disturbing event or the time following the event that makes me feel appreciation or gratitude?" For example, did someone protect you, help you, or enrich your life somehow? Is there part of you that protected yourself from further harm? Do you still have friends, love, or hope? Have you perhaps discovered the ability to respond with greater self-compassion?

- Did you hear unkind or negative messages during or afterward? Did the event cause you to replay old critical messages you might have heard from parents or others? Could you replace such messages with compassionate responses? Instead of "You're not good enough," "You're a failure," or "Why are you so stupid!" you might say to yourself, "That was difficult. I did my best. Next time I'll probably be wiser." You might give yourself a hug as you say these kinder statements.

- Affirm the present strengths of your mind, body, and spirit. Identify times when you survived or showed strength, such as perseverance, wisdom, determination, or wise decision making.

- Describe the path ahead. How will these past events guide your thoughts and actions in the future?

CHAPTER 26

An Overview of Unconditional Love

In this section of the book, we have explored some very important ideas and skills related to the second building block of self-esteem, unconditional love. Because this factor is so important, let's review some of the key ideas and skills.

Supportive Ideas

1. Love for one's core self is a wholesome feeling. It is also the attitude of wanting what is best for oneself, and a decision that is made daily.

2. Psychological health and growth depend on love for the core.

3. Love is learned and acquired through practice.

4. One is responsible for cultivating love for the core self. One can count on this love, even if one cannot count on love from others.

Acquired Skills

1. Find, love, and heal the core self

2. Kind descriptions and changing channels

3. Circle of differing gifts

4. Acknowledge and accept positive qualities

5. Cultivate body appreciation

6. Reinforce and strengthen body appreciation

7. Utilize the *even though…nevertheless* skill

8. Eyes of love meditation

9. Liking the face in the mirror

10. See yourself through loving eyes

11. Experience love at the heart level

12. Be mindfully aware of suffering

13. Basic self-compassion meditation

14. Experience self-compassion at the body level

15. Compassionate journaling

To reinforce these important ideas and skills, please take a few moments to respond to the following questions. You might first wish to flip back through the preceding pages of this section to review what you've done.

1. The ideas about factor II that have had the most meaning to me are:

2. The skills that I would most like to remember and use are:

3. What do I need more of regarding factor II exercises? Are there certain skills that I would like to practice more? (Set aside as long of a period of time as you need to practice them.)

The Active Side of Love: Growing

CHAPTER 27

The Basics of Growing

Every decision we make is a statement of how much we value ourselves.
—US Army Chaplain N. Alden Brown

Self-esteem is as much a matter of the heart as it is of cognition. This is especially true for the third building block of self-esteem, growing. Other names for growing include

- love in action,

- completing,

- coming to flower, and

- the *even more* factor.

The *even more* factor derives from my most beloved teacher. Tall and gangly, some would say that he was not particularly handsome. In fact, some would say he was not good looking at all. But he knew his mother loved him, and so everybody liked him. He related that he acquired his first suit, a blue one, at nineteen years of age. And when he put on that blue suit with a clean white shirt and a tie, thinking about how he was going to teach and serve others, he said—and his face lit up as he related this—"I became *even more* handsome!"

Factor III, growing, is the calm feeling of being *even more* of what you are at the core. In other words, *growing* is developing the traits that exist in embryo. You feel deeply and quietly glad to be who you are because you know that you are being the best person you can be—at the reasonable and steady pace that is uniquely suited to you.

In short, then, growing means

- developing our capacities and potentialities;

- ascending, and moving toward excellence; and

- elevating humanity, both others and the self.

We have likened the core self to a crystal of infinite, unchanging worth—with every needed attribute in embryo. Factor I, unconditional human worth, accurately sees this. Factor II, unconditional love, strengthens and shines the core and provides the foundation for factor III, growing.

Growing, or completing, involves scrubbing off the remaining dirt and lifting the core into the light, where it may shine even more brightly. As this drawing suggests, the core always has worth, but when we bring it into the light, it is more fully enjoyed.

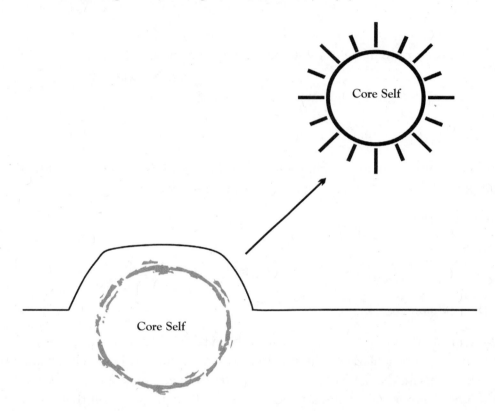

Love in Action: The Next Steps

Having already removed the cognitive distortions that can camouflage or dirty the core, the next tasks are to

- choose behaviors that are loving and self-promoting, and

- remove behaviors from around the core that are not loving, because they are not self-promoting. These include any practices that are unhealthy or unkind, including drug use, excessive anger, sex that objectifies, sleeping too little, eating too much food, and inhaling too much nicotine.

Personal growth is one of life's greatest pleasures. To repeat, self-esteem does not mean complacency. Hafen (1989) notes that some advance

> the misleading idea that self-acceptance is the end of therapeutic or personal development rather than the beginning. Counseling can in this way become less concerned with assisting people toward change and more concerned with simply helping them to be more comfortable. That might be an adequate approach for helping someone come to terms with having a terminal illness; but it is unlikely to succeed as well in aiding the process of personal growth and development.

So self-esteem—the realistic, appreciative opinion of oneself—rests on the combination of self-acceptance (factors I and II) and coming to flower (factor III).

"Dennis the Menace" used by permission of Hank Ketcham Enterprises and North American Syndicate.

Perspectives on Growing

Factor III—the healthy growing process—rests on the following ten principles.

1. We are designed and created to develop physically, mentally, socially, emotionally, and spiritually—and will do so when our capacities are nourished and exercised. The nourishment is love.

2. Developing our capacities is a way of loving ourselves. Sharing them is a way of loving others.

3. Growing is an *outgrowth* of unconditional worth and unconditional love, not a *condition* for these. Love provides the soil for growth. If a sense of unconditional worth and love is absent, success, performance, and producing rarely lead to self-esteem. Therefore, the decision to develop is best preceded by factors I and II.

4. Growing does not mean a high degree of competence, because

    •   research indicates that competence does not predict global self-esteem, and

    •   "competence," as it is usually used, implies an outcome (for example, accomplished, finished, perfected).

    Rather, growing is a perception that says

    •   "I can" (for example, "I am capable and have ability."), and

    •   "I am on track and moving in a desired direction."

    So growing is a *direction* and a *process*, not an outcome. Thus, one can feel good about progress, even if one falls short of a desired goal (for example, perfection).

5. Developing our capacities does not change, increase, or prove worth (worth exists at birth, already infinite and unchanging). Rather, as we grow we express our worth; we change our perceptions of self; we experience ourselves with more joy, appreciation, and satisfaction; we see our true, core selves more clearly; and we put ourselves in the sunlight where the core self shines more brightly.

6. Over time, good experiences with a friend solidify our trust and favorable opinions of that friend. Similarly, good experiences with our self fix and enhance self-appreciation.

7. Growing is an ongoing process. Unlike the rose, which blooms and then dies, the core self can continue to grow even as the outer shell ages.

8. Growth is not completed in isolation but is accomplished interdependently (for example, with the help of others, nature, or grace).

9. Growing consists simply of cultivating *integrity* (moral conduct and character) and *wholesome pleasure* (that is, pleasure that re-creates without compromising conscience,

including pursuits such as art, beauty, hobbies, learning, developing talents, serving, cleaning and beautifying surroundings, playing, working, and loving).

10. People choose to grow or develop so they can be happier. As we become happier, we tend to enjoy life and ourselves more.

Questions Regarding Growth

Are integrity and pleasure somehow incompatible? Integrity implies integration or wholeness. It implies that there is no division between one's behavior and one's values. When we develop integrity, we experience ourselves with more peace and can say, along with Winslow Homer, "All is lovely outside my house and inside my house and myself." Moral behavior becalms, and it is kind, peaceable, and honest. Integrity is developed by starting the day with the decision to *put integrity first.*

Although some argue that pleasure is somehow incompatible with integrity, recall that the canonized Catholic saint Thomas Aquinas said, "No man can live without delight, and that is why a man deprived of joy of the spirit [for example, joy of living, joie de vivre] goes over into carnal pleasures."

Gandhi further explained that it is not pleasure that corrupts the consciousness but pleasure without conscience (that is, pleasures that exploit, abuse, or violate trust). *Wholesome* pleasure is re-creative and necessary. Only the pleasures that degrade the human consciousness are to be avoided. In this sense, the pursuit of wholesome pleasure is consistent with the pursuit of integrity.

To have self-esteem, must I have perfect integrity? Inner peace requires that one is doing the best that one knows how. One can do no more than one knows how to do or is capable of doing. Since everyone is fallible, each person falls short of perfection. However, we can still experience our worth if we try our best to be on course and to be moving in the desired direction.

When is growing not fun? Growing is not fun when the outcome becomes a dire necessity. If, for example, one *must* develop into a successful salesperson as a condition of worth or happiness, then one will likely feel driven, not joyful. Again, we return to the fact that wholesome growing assumes that unconditional worth and love are first in place, so that one can enjoy the *process* of growing without fear of failure or preoccupation with the outcome. Preoccupation with outcome and fear of failure both derive from the same roots: *conditional* worth and *conditional* love.

Growing is like climbing the staircase, not arriving. Thus, one can enjoy the progress and the direction without feeling frustration for failing to arrive at perfection.

Reflections on Elevating Humanity and the Self

Factor III is a pleasant, satisfying reaching—reaching beyond one's present level of development, and reaching out to others—as these reflections suggest. Please take time now to ponder them.

Once you have a self [that is, you are secure in your own worth], then it is easier to lose yourself in selfless service.

—Anonymous

If I am not for myself, who will be for me? But if I am only for myself, what am I?

—Hillel

I discovered that if I worked always and only for all humanity, I would be optimally effective.

—Buckminster Fuller

The great failure of education is that it has made people tribe-conscious rather than species-conscious.

—Norman Cousins

The great use of life is to spend it for something that will outlast it.

—William James

One knows from daily life that one exists for other people.... A hundred times each day I remind myself.

—Albert Einstein

He could have added fortune to fame, but caring for neither, he found happiness and honor in being helpful to the world.

—Written as George Washington Carver's epitaph

The desire to elevate humanity—the self, another person, all others—is what in everyday language we call love. Love is wanting the very best for the object of our love.

—John Burt

166

If you have weaknesses, try and overcome them, and if you fail, try again, and if you then fail, keep trying, for God is merciful to His children. He is a good deal kinder to us than we are to ourselves.

—J. Golden Kimball

If all else fails, try doing something nice for someone who doesn't expect it. You'll be surprised how good you'll feel.

—George Burns

If you could follow this…rule [your mild depression] would be cured in fourteen days. It is—to consider from time to time how you can give another person [wholesome] pleasure….. You would feel yourself to be useful and worthwhile.

—Alfred Adler

No man need fear death, he need fear only that he may die without having known his greatest power—the power of his free will to give his life for others.

—Albert Schweitzer

[We are all] craftsmen, investing our talents.

—Laura Benet

As we see what we can do we more fully appreciate who we are.

—Anonymous

Service is an eye toward others' lasting development.

—Dallin H. Oaks

The only way the magic [that is, growth] works is by hard work. But hard work can be fun.

—Jim Henson, Muppets creator

Some say principles are constraining. I say they are liberating. Some say service is subservience. But I say it is ennobling.

—Anonymous

167

CHAPTER 28

Accept That You Aren't Perfect

Growing is like climbing a mountain. If you know you have firm footing, then you push up with confidence, and it's fun. Factors I and II are the firm footings of growth. As you set out to grow and to enjoy the process, some people might "rain on your parade" by reminding you in one way or another that you and your efforts are less than perfect. The following *nevertheless* skill varies slightly from the previous two versions:

Even though I am not perfect, nevertheless _____.
(some statement of growing)

For example, if someone tells you that you can't do anything right, you might say or think:

"*Even though I'm not perfect, nevertheless* I'm growing."

Other *nevertheless* statements:

- I'm sure trying.

- I'm learning.

- I'm on course and moving along.

- I'm still new at this and finding my way.

- I still enjoy trying.

- I think I can improve.

- My worth is infinite, I appreciate my efforts, and I have as much right to try as anybody.

- I still "work."

- I'm having fun.

- I'm developing in other ways.

- Learning is still adventurous.

- I'm more (kind, of a person, etc.) today than I was yesterday.

- I still persist and get it done.

Can you think of others that you like?

Even Though I'm Not Perfect…Nevertheless: An Exercise

Select a partner. Ask your partner to say whatever negative statements come to mind, be they true or false, such as:

- My frog has a quicker wit than you do!

- Singing lessons? *You!?*

- Your lousy memory lost us that account!

- You'll never amount to much!

- Why are you so slow?

- Your personality bugs me!

To each criticism, put your ego on the shelf, and respond with an *even though I'm not perfect…nevertheless* statement. Try to keep your sense of humor and respond with an upbeat feeling.

Accept Your Imperfections: An Exercise

1. For each of the next six days, select three events or situations with the potential to erode self-esteem.

2. In response to each one, select an *even though I'm not perfect…nevertheless* statement. Then, on the worksheet below, describe the event or situation, the statement you used, and the emotional effect you experience from selecting this statement and saying it to yourself. Keeping a written record reinforces the skill:

Date	Event/Situation	Statement Used	Effect
1. 2. 3.			
1. 2. 3.			
1. 2. 3.			
1. 2. 3.			
1. 2. 3.			
1. 2. 3.			

CHAPTER 29

Just for the Fun of It
(Contemplating Possibilities)

Jim Henson, the creator of the Muppets, was appreciated widely for his childlike qualities, meaning the enjoyable and precious qualities of a child. Consider the following childlike qualities:

- Sense of discovery, wonder, curiosity
- Vulnerability
- Warmth
- Sympathetic
- Appreciative
- Enthusiastic
- Responsive
- Zestful
- Trusting
- Capacities to (Montegu 1988):
  - Learn
  - Live
  - Grow
  - Imagine, fantasize, dream

- Experiment

- Explore

- Be open-minded

- Love

- Work

- Play

- Think

Although the storms of life might diminish the flames of some of these qualities, the ember of each quality is never entirely extinguished. A beauty of maturity is that one often has acquired the wisdom and emotional security to cultivate these qualities again.

A Brief Inventory

Please record your responses to the following questions.

1. What do you like about your personality? (Recognizing strengths is a way of loving yourself.)

2. Answer the question "What would you like to improve?" using the following format: It's true that I sometimes _____ , so I'd like to be more _____ .
                    (describe behavior)   (describe quality)

There is no shame in having rough edges. However, notice the positive emotional tone of matter-of-factly acknowledging reality, while also noticing possibilities.

Attractive and Appealing Qualities

Proverbs 29:18 states, "Where there is no vision, the people perish." This exercise might help you begin to create a vision, or pleasant pathway, toward personal growth.

What qualities of character increase a person's attractiveness or appeal? Psychologist J. Brothers (1990) suggests the following traits are characteristics of older people whom others experience as attractive and appealing. One could argue that these characteristics apply to people of all ages, including you.

1. Put a check beside a trait if you agree that it would increase a person's attractiveness or appeal.

   ☐ Cheerful

   ☐ Poised

   ☐ Aware

   ☐ Delights in the senses (enjoys food, nature, and so forth)

   ☐ Interested in all people

   ☐ Enthusiastic about life

   ☐ Upbeat (not critical of others or self)

   ☐ Healthy and vigorous (conditioned, hygienic)

   ☐ Inner strength (learns from mistakes without agonizing over them)

   ☐ Vulnerability (feels, accepts own faults)

   ☐ Relates to people as individuals (notices, smiles at, talks to, offers thanks)

   ☐ Kind

   ☐ Good

   ☐ Focuses on assets, not shortcomings

   ☐ Fun (has fun, is fun, sometimes flirts for fun)

   ☐ Expresses male and female sides (is flexible)

   ☐ Enjoys friendships with both sexes (sees individuals as whole and complex)

2. Are there other traits you would add to the list? What are they?

3. If you were to select four traits that you might wish to develop—for yourself, just for the fun of it—what would they be?

    a.

    b.

    c.

    d.

CHAPTER 30

Take Stock of Your Character

Self-esteem is not an exercise in positive thinking, in which you tell yourself how wonderful and perfect you are, hoping that you will thereby become so. This kind of thinking is emotionally immature and stressful because it is not grounded in reality. People with self-esteem have no need to inflate themselves. Rather they are secure enough to accurately appraise both their strengths and weaknesses. Growth begins with an honest recognition of one's present level of development. The process can be quite self-affirming and optimistic when done with genuine regard for the core self.

The following activity is based on the moral inventory used in Alcoholics Anonymous (AA). AA members teach that when a grocer inventories the shelves, he just counts what's there and what isn't. He does not judge; he just counts. When we inventory our own shelves, we simply count, without judging the core self.

This activity is called the loving, fearless, searching, honest moral inventory. It is *loving* because love casts out fear. With love, and without fear, we simply acknowledge where we presently stand. Fear results when a person negatively judges his or her core. What would be more frightening than concluding that one is bad to the core? The label "bad" is irrational because it implies that one is totally and always bad. The more realistic view is that one is infinitely worthwhile at the core but also possesses some rough edges. The inventory is *honest* and *moral* because we honestly search and identify both strengths and weaknesses. If we only found weaknesses, it would be called an "*immoral* inventory." We consider something to be moral if it is in the long-term best interests of humankind, immoral if it is not.

The inventory will follow the BASIC MID pattern adapted from psychologist Arnold Lazarus's (1984) multimodal approach to helping. This approach assumes that people have strengths and weaknesses in eight dimensions of their lives, each dimension being represented by a letter in the acronym BASIC MID (behavior, affect, sensations, imagery, cognitions, moral, interpersonal, drugs/biology). Seeing strengths and weaknesses side-by-side helps put our weaknesses in perspective. That is, we see weak areas as rough edges that can be strengthened and developed—smoothed and polished. They are not representative of the whole core. Related to each BASIC MID dimension are ways to grow and develop. Remember, acknowledging present reality can clarify your direction and goals.

A List of Moral Strengths

Do you quietly, but honestly, give yourself credit for the good you try to do? Or, do you mini-mize your efforts? It can be very helpful to take a fresh look at your strengths, perhaps recog-nizing inner resources that you undervalue or take for granted. In this spirit, I'd like you to make an inventory of your strengths. Below are listed a number of qualities that could be considered moral strengths because they contribute to the best interests of humankind, includ-ing self.

1. Please check all the qualities below that you, to a reasonable degree (that is, not demand-ing perfection), demonstrate.

   ☐ Integrity

   ☐ Compassion

   ☐ Love

   ☐ Virtue

   ☐ Knowledge

   ☐ Patience

   ☐ Kindness

   ☐ Humility or willingness to admit faults

   ☐ Respect for others

   ☐ Respect for self

   ☐ Honesty

   ☐ Helpfulness

   ☐ Supportiveness

   ☐ Affection

   ☐ Consideration or thoughtfulness

   ☐ Tolerance for diversity

- ☐ Trust
- ☐ Moral cleanliness
- ☐ A sense of duty or responsibility
- ☐ Care for your reputation
- ☐ Forgiveness
- ☐ Friendliness
- ☐ Penitence or appropriate sorrow
- ☐ Hope or optimism
- ☐ Thriftiness
- ☐ Selflessness or service
- ☐ Sharing
- ☐ Gentleness
- ☐ Civility or courtesy
- ☐ Thankfulness
- ☐ Appreciation
- ☐ Dependability or keeping to your word

2. Circle an item above if developing it more fully would further your growth or happiness.

Assessing Eight Areas of Living

On the BASIC MID checkup and planning sheet that follows, you will assess your life in the following eight areas. Keep in mind, you are looking for general patterns. Certainly, most of us will at times experience many of the weaknesses mentioned.

1. **Behavior** includes things you do—acts, habits, gestures, or reactions. Strengths might include punctuality, a pleasant expression, cleanliness, budgeting time for recreation, steadiness, measured speech, attractive dress, good grooming, or accomplishing tasks at work. Weaknesses might include avoiding or withdrawing from challenges, procrastinating, frowning or grimacing, a defeated posture, being disorganized, controlling people, yelling, the silent treatment, compulsive behaviors, and impatient or reckless driving behavior.

2. **Affect** refers to feelings you experience. Strengths could include optimism, peace, appreciation of self, contentment with what you have, cheerfulness, or calmness. Problems might include chronic depression, anxiety, anger, worry, fear, guilt, or self-dislike.

3. **Sensations** refer to the five senses. Strengths might include enjoying the wind, tastes, smells, sounds, and sights. Problems, or symptoms of problems, might be chronic headaches, tension, nausea, dizziness, stomach tightness, or seeing only negatives in the environment and not the beautiful.

4. **Imagery** refers to the scenes that play out in your mind. Strengths might be visualizing a pleasant future vacation, having pleasant dreams, or experiencing a pleasant feeling upon seeing one's reflection. Negatives might include nightmares, seeing oneself failing, a faulty self-image, or focusing on the negatives in the mirror.

5. **Cognitions** deal with our thoughts. Strengths are indicated by realistic optimism (that is, *not everything will be perfect, but I'll find something to enjoy, grow from, or improve*); cognitive skills, such as the *nevertheless* skills (see chapters 6, 17, and 28); or cognitive rehearsal (see chapter 14). Problems are indicated by the presence of distortions.

6. **Moral** refers to one's character and conduct. Strengths include any of the qualities listed previously. Weaknesses would be the opposites.

7. **Interpersonal** describes the quality of relationships. Strengths include having good intimate relationships, making family and friends a high priority, affiliating with people other than coworkers, and so on. Weaknesses include the absence of friends, aggression (for example, name-calling, violence, or sarcasm), consistently withdrawing from people who disappoint you, or nonassertiveness (for example, allowing oneself to be used).

8. **Drugs/biology** refers to present health habits. Habits that reflect self-regard, and are therefore strengths, include adequate rest and relaxation, regular exercise, and proper nutrition. Junk food, chronic use of tranquilizers or sleeping pills, smoking, or drug abuse generally reflect a disregard for one's health and oneself.

The Loving, Fearless, Searching, and Honest Moral Inventory

1. Under each of the eight areas on the BASIC MID checkup and planning sheet, list present strengths or what is presently going well in your life.

2. What are the present problem areas in your life? What do you notice that dissatisfies you? Describe these under "present weaknesses (symptoms/problems)" for each of the BASIC MID areas.

3. As you review the present weak areas in your life, how would your life be different if you were to develop these areas? Describe your life in each of the eight areas. For example, if I were less anxious, what would I see or hear differently? How would relationships be different?

4. Under each of the BASIC MID areas, indicate what you could do to change or grow. Please note that you suggest possibilities in order to reinforce strengths and to develop areas that are presently weaker. This can require your best creative thinking. There are many, many ways to develop, just as a weak muscle can be strengthened by a variety of exercises. For example, to improve health habits, one could read up on the subject, join a health club, hire a nutritionist, or initiate a walking program with senior citizens. To reduce symptoms of anxiety, one could learn breathing control and muscle relaxation, or seek assistance from a skilled mental health professional. One could reduce excessive anger by uprooting distortions, restoring self-esteem, applying healing skills, and learning to forgive. You can make many steps toward growth and development by yourself. Recognizing when help is needed and finding that help are signs of healthy self-esteem.

   Some interesting realizations arise in completing this exercise. For example, is alcoholism a moral problem? It is not if one views it as an addiction and refuses to judge the core of the addicted individual. It is if you consider that the *behavior* adversely affects the individual and his or her family. Do you, then, place alcoholism under "drugs/biology" or under "moral"? In my view, this is not a critical issue. The purpose of the inventory is to help you increase awareness of areas that are affecting your life, for good or bad. Because there can be overlap among the eight categories, it is not critical in which category a strength or weakness appears. What matters is only that you acknowledge them, and that you refuse to judge or condemn the core, because you recognize that you are imperfect.

   Take your time completing the inventory. You may wish to complete it over a three-day period, allowing time for rest and contemplation.

5. Select one entry from step four above, one with which you feel reasonably confident about making progress and finding enjoyment and satisfaction in the process. For a week, do what you need to do in order to progress in this area.

6. Resolve to return to this inventory each month to see where you are in relation to step four and to consider new goals.

Growth does not happen overnight. Some feel disappointed when it does not. Returning to the self-as-a-portrait analogy, it is helpful to think that a classic painting takes years to complete. In this case, however, the portrait is never finished; its evolution is an ongoing process.

BASIC MID Checkup and Planning Sheet

(The Loving, Fearless, Searching, and Honest Moral Inventory)

Behavior	Affect	Sensations	Imagery	Cognitions	Moral (conduct and character)	Interpersonal	Drugs/Biology
			Present Strengths				
		Present Weaknesses (Symptoms/Problems)					
	How Would My Life Be Different If I Developed My Weaker Areas?						
			What I Could Do to Change/Grow				

CHAPTER 31

Practice Forgiving

[There is] no future without forgiveness.

—Desmond Tutu

He who has not forgiven an enemy has never yet tasted one of the most sublime enjoyments of life.

—Robert Lauter

In my community lives a courageous young immigrant named Tran. As a young boy in Vietnam, Tran lived in poverty, under a rock. Seeking a better life for him, his mother placed him in foster care in the United States. In his foster home, Tran was severely abused. When he reached his teen years, Tran told his abuser that he had forgiven him and wished the best for him. Looking back on that troubled period of his life, Tran reflected, "Forgiving is replacing anger with love. Forgiving freed me to move on with my life."

The German philosopher Friedrich Nietzsche suggested that only the weak forgive. The research, however, suggests that it is really the wise and courageous who forgive.

Robert D. Enright, whose writings inspire much of the material in this chapter, is the trailblazer in forgiveness research. Studying diverse populations of all ages—survivors of trauma, incest, abuse, and drug addiction; men hurt by the abortion decision of a partner; elderly women; cancer and cardiac patients; children in Northern Ireland—he found that practicing forgiveness consistently led to improved mental health, including improved self-esteem and more efficiently functioning hearts. Even fairly small improvements in forgiving led to substantial psychological improvements.

What Is Forgiveness?

Enright defines forgiveness as "a process, freely chosen by you, in which you willingly reduce resentment through some hard work and offer goodness of some kind toward the one who hurt you" (2012, 49). Let's look at some of the key elements of this definition:

- **Process.** Forgiving serious offenses usually does not come quickly, easily, or all at once.

- **Choice.** No one can force us to forgive. We forgive when we are ready. The choice to forgive does not depend on whether the offender apologizes, deserves to be forgiven, or changes. The choice simply relates to how we decide to respond to the past.

- **Resentment.** This is feeling the original anger again. When we forgive, we choose to release bitterness and the intent to get even so that we can be freed of the heavy burden that keeps us chained to the past and sours our present life.

- **Offering goodness to the offender.** Releasing ill will, judgments, and vengeance toward the offender is a healing place to start. Offering compassion to the offender is even more healing. Perhaps we start by avoiding or tolerating the offender, refusing to speak ill of him, or doing him no harm. Over time and after needed healing, we might cultivate kind thoughts toward the offender. We remember that everyone is imperfect and suffers, and that the offender's hurtful actions will inevitably diminish his happiness. The response we choose is to love and respect the offender, despite her behaviors—even though we dislike those behaviors. Perhaps a smile replaces anger or indifference. Perhaps we eventually wish the person well or actively seek to serve the offender.

What Forgiving Is Not

1. Forgiving is not minimizing the hurt or ignoring your anger. Paradoxically, dismissing the pain or breezily offering forgiveness too quickly can impede your attempts to heal. It is acknowledging pain and touching it with compassion that heals.

2. Forgiving does not mean trusting or reconciling with the offender. Rebuilding damaged relationships takes time and trust. The offender might not be deserving of your trust. We can forgive with or without reconciling.

3. Forgiving does not mean tolerating bad behavior or allowing it to continue. Sometimes the loving course is to bring an offender to justice to prevent her from repeating behaviors that are self-destructive or harmful to others. However, this can be done with determined concern, not bitterness.

4. Forgiveness is not forgetting, only changing our response to the past. We treat others as we'd wish to be treated, regardless of how we were treated. We offer honor and respect even if the offender did not honor and respect us.

How Does Forgiving Lift Self-Esteem?

Loving the offender puts you in touch with your best self—your true, loving nature. As you drop the chains of resentment that keep you tied to the past, the heart that has been closed off with anger can reopen. Forgiving is a three-way gift of goodness, one that feels good to give. Forgiveness is a gift to (Enright 2001):

1. **The offender.** Forgiveness recognizes that the offender has worth that runs deeper than his behavior. Treating the offender with love and respect, even when this is not immediately appreciated, can sometimes soften the offender's heart and inspire him to become his best self. A desire to lift all people, even those who behave badly, is an important aspect of growing.

2. **The self.** Even if the offender doesn't accept forgiveness, you will likely benefit by the act of forgiving. Perhaps you will experience less resentment and cynicism and more happiness. Perhaps choosing to place love in your heart will make you feel more whole (Salzberg 1995), more like your old self. Perhaps you'll sleep more peacefully and be able to live more fully in the present. Perhaps in viewing the humanity that you share with the offender, you will also grow more compassionate toward yourself. Perhaps you'll realize that the offender is no longer controlling your life—you are! The goal of forgiving is not to just change a response to an isolated offense but to become a more forgiving, more loving person—both important aspects of growing.

3. **Others.** Anger that is bottled up often gets passed on to others, including family members—sometimes for generations—until we forgive. Practicing forgiveness can help us to be less critical, impatient, and judgmental of others at home and in general. Such practices can help us experience both ourselves and others more positively.

The How of Forgiving

To begin, consider whether or not forgiveness is needed, and for what offenses.

Assess

Do you need to forgive? The need to forgive might be tipped off by any of the following symptoms. Check those that apply to you.

☐ Anger (at life, family, authority figures, people who remind you of the offender, and so forth) that is smoldering or excessive, erupts irrationally, or spills out onto others

☐ Feeling victimized or betrayed; blaming your life circumstances on the past

☐ Holding grudges or resentments; obsessing or ruminating about getting even or hurting the offender; fuming

☐ Sour mood (cynical, depressed, negative, pessimistic, critical, distrustful, unhappy, defensive)

☐ Complaining (life is unfair, nothing is good enough)

☐ Sarcasm

☐ Guilt (for something you did or failed to do, for not forgiving, or for harboring ill will)

☐ Anxiety, fear

☐ Fatigue, tension

☐ Dreams about the offense

☐ Feeling devalued; having lowered self-esteem

☐ Avoiding people, withdrawing to avoid further wounding, or sulking

☐ Sedating pain (with alcohol, drugs, shopping, gambling, risky behaviors, excessive sleep)

☐ Sensitivity to criticism

Identify Unresolved Offenses from the Past

List offenses and who committed them (for example, parents, children, relatives, friends, partners, teachers, colleagues, authority figures, religious community, neighbors). Offenses might include the following:

Withdrawing love—rejection, neglect, abandonment, death, infidelity _____

_____

_____

Emotional, physical, or sexual abuse _____

_____

_____

Unintentional hurts _____

_____

_____

Criticism, impatience, blaming, being yelled at or scolded _____

_____

_____

Humiliation or embarrassment _____

_____

_____

Prejudice _____

_____

_____

Betrayal by political leaders _____

_____

_____

Life's unfairness _____

_____

_____

God _____

_____

_____

Other(s) _____

_____

_____

Tools for Forgiving

This section describes three helpful approaches to forgiving: two forgiveness journaling exercises and a forgiveness meditation.

Forgiveness Journaling

We cannot heal wounds that we do not acknowledge. You might start by writing about a single offense, perhaps beginning with a smaller one. Without judging, write simply to gain understanding and express feelings so that you can eventually move past the offense. Try writing about:

- **The facts surrounding what happened.** Who was the offender? Was the offense intentional?

- **The effects the offense has had on your life.** With an accepting attitude, acknowledge the resulting feelings (anger, shame, numbing, and so forth), loss of innocence or other losses, changed views of people and the world, physical sensations or illness, and so on.

- **Connections to earlier wounds.** Does this offense remind you of earlier offenses that perhaps triggered similar feelings or outcomes?

- **The offender's condition.** Henry Wadsworth Longfellow wrote, "If we could read the secret history of our enemies we should find in each man's life sorrow and suffering enough to disarm all hostility." There is suffering in *every* person's life. Might the offender have been worse off than you assumed? Might the offender have been experiencing her own hurt or insecurity at the time of the offense? Might he have been carrying wounds from a difficult past or been oblivious to the suffering of others?

Neff suggests considering these questions (2011, 199): "What happened to make them lose touch with their hearts? What wound occurred to lead to such cold and callous behavior? What's *their* story?" You might also wish to write about the following: Might the offender be worse off now than you assume? People who are happy and in their right mind do not intentionally hurt others. Those who harm others inevitably suffer themselves. How might she be suffering from hurting you or others (for example, earning the distrust or dislike of others, worrying about punishment, diminishing her self-respect)? Why is the offender worthwhile, despite the bad behavior?

- **Your possible role.** Did you contribute to the offense with your reactions at the time? Are you in need of forgiveness for something you did or did not do, or for holding on to judgment and anger? Might you need to forgive yourself? (The principles of forgiving yourself are the same as for forgiving another.)

- **Committing to forgive.** When you realize that holding on to grudges is not working, you determine to try a different approach, to begin the difficult process of forgiving. You decide to release resentment so that you and those around you will suffer less. You accept that offenders (including yourself) are imperfect, and you release yourself from the role of the sheriff who must punish all infractions. You strive, however imperfectly, to replace unfairness with kindness. You commit to the work it takes to release the burden you've carried for too long. You might specify what you will now do and not do. (For example, "I commit, as best I can, to release anger toward the offender. I will say something kind about him; I'll remind myself that his core worth is deeper and greater than his actions—that he and I have equal worth. I will wish for and take delight in his happiness.")

Perhaps you remind yourself that your core worth is not changed, even though you were dishonored! As Enright (2012) explains, in bearing the pain without retaliating or transferring it to others, you are giving a gift of love to the world, ending the cycle of wounding and hate, as Gandhi, Martin Luther King Jr., and Mother Teresa did. This gift takes extraordinary love—for yourself, realizing that your worth has not changed, and for the offender, realizing there is more to him as a person than his behavior. This takes great strength and courage and sets an example that can inspire others (such as our children). Don't be discouraged if strong, negative feelings arise during the forgiveness process (for example, "I want to wring his neck!"). Simply try to bring kindness to the offender, as best you can. Allow time for your feelings to gradually shift.

- **The possible good that did or could still occur as a result of this offense.** Did you discover that you are strong enough to absorb hurt without retaliating? Are you more aware of the need to forgive yourself? To be kinder to yourself and others who make mistakes? To be more compassionate to fallible human beings? Have you acquired new ways to heal? To mend relationships?

Forgiveness Meditation

Try this powerful meditation (Salzberg 1995, 75), which, with daily practice, helps to replace unkind feelings with kind ones.

1. **Sit comfortably.** Close your eyes, if that is comfortable, and breathe abdominally. Allow time to reflect without rushing through this meditation.

2. **Ask for forgiveness of others.** Recite silently or aloud, whichever you prefer, "If I have hurt or harmed anyone, knowingly or unknowingly, I ask their forgiveness." As different people, images, or scenarios arise in awareness, release the burden of guilt and repeat, "I ask your forgiveness."

3. **Offer forgiveness to others.** Repeat silently or aloud, whichever you prefer, "If anyone has hurt or harmed me, knowingly or unknowingly, I forgive them." For whatever image comes up, repeat "I forgive you."

4. **Offer forgiveness to yourself.** Reflect on anything you have done to harm yourself or others, for any unloving acts, including the inability to forgive. Recite silently or aloud, "For all of the ways I have hurt or harmed myself, knowingly or unknowingly, I offer forgiveness."

As you sit quietly, ponder this: How does it feel to ask for and experience forgiveness? How does it feel to offer forgiveness to others? How might the regular practice of forgiving benefit you? Later, in your journal, you might further explore these questions, as well as the following:

- Has writing about your pain caused it to shift in any way?

- Does forgiving bring greater feelings of inner strength, confidence, freedom from the past, and happiness than does avoiding your pain or seeking revenge?

- Are you better able to handle inner pain than you thought?

Considerations

1. Remember, you don't have to forgive. It might not be wise to forgive before you are ready. You might instead think, *I wish to forgive, and will do so eventually, but right now I am not ready.* You might first need some time and healing.

2. Forgiving might be a process of two steps forward and one back. If feelings of anger resurface, this does not invalidate your progress. Keep trying.

3. Carefully consider whether or not it is in your best interest to meet with an offender. The offender may not be physically available or may lack the emotional maturity to hear and respond respectfully to your pain. In such cases, consider simply writing out your thoughts and feelings without sharing them with the offender.

When You Have Caused Suffering

Asking for forgiveness—when we courageously acknowledge our mistakes and seek to soothe the hurt of another person—is an act of strength, humility, and kindness. You might try writing in your journal with kind acceptance and without judgment about hurt you've caused (Pennebaker and Evans 2014).

- Acknowledge your role—what you did imperfectly.

- Carefully think about the events leading up to the offense—your thoughts and feelings prior to, during, and after.

- Consider the other person's feelings and thoughts before, during, and after. Consider the impact on the person and her family and friends. Think about how you would have felt if the same event had happened to you. If you can, express sorrow.

- An apology can be healing. Write out an apology, perhaps using statements similar to the following (Enright 2001):

    - I'm so sorry for hurting you. Please forgive me.

    - It wasn't my intent to hurt you.

    - Is there anything I can do to make it up to you?

    - I was wrong. I'm sorry. Please forgive me.

- Explore what might help you make amends to the offended person.

Summary of Forgiving

As Tran said, forgiving is replacing hatred with love. We forgive because loving is at the core of who we are. Forgiving shows inner strength that is independent of others' behaviors; it's a choice we make even though people disrespect and dishonor us. Not forgiving hurts ourselves and others by keeping hatred alive, closing our hearts to love, and spreading anger to others.

Forgiving helps to heal and open the heart so that we can be our true selves again. In forgiving, we see others as wounded, just as we have been, and respond to pain with compassion. Thus, we are responding from our true best self. Forgiving says, "I'm still here, still standing, still loving, refusing to be diminished by your acts."

When we commit an offense, forgiving says, "I forgive myself because I know I am more than my mistakes; I believe I will improve more with kindness than with self-condemnation."

CHAPTER 32

Experience Wholesome Pleasure

The greatest challenge of life is how to enjoy it.

—Nathaniel Branden

The average American adult, employed full time, works forty-seven hours per week according to a 2014 Gallup survey (Saad), leaving little time for leisure. People tend to give up activities that give them pleasure when they're short on time (Lewinsohn et al. 1986). As a result of the stress and the absence of pleasure, their mood slips. The more depressed people become, the more their self-esteem erodes, and the less likely they are to believe that formerly enjoyable activities will bring them pleasure. So they fail to engage in the satisfying activities that would lift their mood and rebuild their self-esteem.

In the absence of leisure time, it becomes more difficult to define yourself apart from your job or paycheck. Harvard economist Juliet Schor (1991) reported that after workers at a British factory were forced to give up overtime because of hard times, a physical and emotional recuperation took place. With time on their hands, including weekends and holidays, friendships developed and the meaning of life became clearer. The allure of money lost some of its intensity. Even those with families to look after preferred the new arrangement, with very few exceptions.

So let's advance the proposition that finding pleasure in life is a skill that adults need to learn, relearn, and reinforce. This skill maintains emotional balance and improves self-esteem by helping us experience ourselves in a variety of pleasant ways. I'm not suggesting that one cannot, or should not, find pleasure in work, only that in the present culture there is a tendency for work to narrowly define an individual. The activity that follows will help you discover, or rediscover, what is pleasant for you, and then make a plan to do some of the things you identify.

Schedule Pleasant Activities

The following activity was developed by Peter Lewinsohn and colleagues (1986).

1. The pleasant events schedule that follows lists a wide range of activities. In column 1, check those activities that you enjoyed in the past. Then rate from 1 to 10 how pleasant each checked item was. A score of 1 reflects little pleasure, and 10 reflects great pleasure. This rating goes in column 1 also, beside each checkmark. For example, if you moderately enjoyed being with happy people but didn't enjoy being with friends or relatives, your first two items would look like this:

    ___√___ (5)   _____ 1. Being with happy people

    _____   _____ 2. Being with friends or relatives

Pleasant Events Schedule

Social interactions are events that occur with others. They tend to make us feel accepted, appreciated, liked, understood, and so forth. You might feel that one of the activities below belongs in another group. Keep in mind that the grouping is not important.

Column 1   **Column 2**

Column 1	Column 2	
_____	_____	1. Being with happy people
_____	_____	2. Being with friends or relatives
_____	_____	3. Thinking about people I like
_____	_____	4. Planning an activity with people I care for
_____	_____	5. Meeting someone new of the same sex
_____	_____	6. Meeting someone new of the opposite sex
_____	_____	7. Going to a club, restaurant, or tavern
_____	_____	8. Being at celebrations (such as birthdays, weddings, baptisms, parties, family get-togethers)
_____	_____	9. Meeting a friend for lunch or a drink

_____ _____ 10. Talking openly and honestly (for example, about my hopes, my fears, what interests me, what makes me laugh, what saddens me)

_____ _____ 11. Expressing true affection (verbal or physical)

_____ _____ 12. Showing interest in others

_____ _____ 13. Noticing successes and strengths in family and friends

_____ _____ 14. Dating and courting (this one is for married individuals, too)

_____ _____ 15. Having a lively conversation

_____ _____ 16. Inviting friends over

_____ _____ 17. Stopping in to visit friends

_____ _____ 18. Calling up someone I enjoy

_____ _____ 19. Apologizing

_____ _____ 20. Smiling at people

_____ _____ 21. Calmly talking over problems with people I live with

_____ _____ 22. Giving compliments, back pats, and praise

_____ _____ 23. Teasing and bantering

_____ _____ 24. Amusing people or making them laugh

_____ _____ 25. Playing with children

_____ _____ 26. Other: _____

Activities that make you feel capable, loving, useful, strong, or adequate

Column 1   **Column 2**

_____   _____   1. Starting a challenging job or doing it well

_____   _____   2. Learning something new (for example, home repair, a hobby, a foreign language)

_____   _____   3. Helping someone (counseling, advising, listening)

_____   _____   4. Contributing to religious, charitable, or other groups

_____   _____   5. Driving skillfully

_____   _____   6. Expressing myself clearly (out loud or in writing)

_____   _____   7. Repairing something (such as sewing, fixing a car or bike)

_____   _____   8. Solving a problem or a puzzle

_____   _____   9. Exercising

_____   _____   10. Thinking

_____   _____   11. Going to a meeting (convention, business, civic)

_____   _____   12. Visiting the ill, homebound, or troubled

_____   _____   13. Telling a child a story

_____   _____   14. Writing a card, note, or letter

_____   _____   15. Improving my appearance (seeking medical or dental help, improving diet, going to a barber or beautician)

_____   _____   16. Planning and budgeting time

_____   _____   17. Discussing political issues

_____   _____   18. Doing volunteer work, community service, or other kind acts

_____ _____ 19. Planning a budget

_____ _____ 20. Protesting injustice, protecting someone, stopping fraud or abuse

_____ _____ 21. Being honest, moral, or having integrity

_____ _____ 22. Correcting mistakes

_____ _____ 23. Organizing a party

_____ _____ 24. Other: _____

Intrinsically pleasant activities

Column 1　　**Column 2**

_____ _____ 1. Laughing

_____ _____ 2. Relaxing, having peace and quiet

_____ _____ 3. Having a good meal

_____ _____ 4. A hobby (cooking, fishing, woodworking, photography, acting, gardening, collecting things)

_____ _____ 5. Listening to good music

_____ _____ 6. Seeing beautiful scenery

_____ _____ 7. Going to bed early, sleeping soundly, and awakening early

_____ _____ 8. Wearing attractive clothes

_____ _____ 9. Wearing comfortable clothes

_____ _____ 10. Going to a concert, opera, ballet, or play

_____ _____ 11. Playing sports (tennis, softball, racquetball, golf, horseshoes, Frisbee)

_____	_____	12. Taking trips or vacations
_____	_____	13. Shopping or buying something I like for myself
_____	_____	14. Being outdoors (beach, country, mountains, kicking leaves, walking in the sand, floating in lakes)
_____	_____	15. Doing artwork (painting, sculpting, drawing)
_____	_____	16. Reading the scriptures or other sacred works
_____	_____	17. Beautifying my home (redecorating, cleaning, yard work, and so forth)
_____	_____	18. Going to a sports event
_____	_____	19. Reading (novels, nonfiction, poems, plays, newspapers)
_____	_____	20. Attending a lecture
_____	_____	21. Taking a drive
_____	_____	22. Sitting in the sun
_____	_____	23. Visiting a museum
_____	_____	24. Playing or singing music
_____	_____	25. Boating
_____	_____	26. Pleasing my family, friends, or employer
_____	_____	27. Thinking about something good in the future
_____	_____	28. Watching TV
_____	_____	29. Camping or hunting
_____	_____	30. Grooming myself (bathing, combing hair, shaving)
_____	_____	31. Writing in my diary or journal

_____	_____	32. Taking a bike ride, hiking, or walking
_____	_____	33. Being with animals
_____	_____	34. Watching people
_____	_____	35. Taking a nap
_____	_____	36. Listening to nature sounds
_____	_____	37. Getting or giving a back rub
_____	_____	38. Watching a storm, clouds, or the sky
_____	_____	39. Having spare time
_____	_____	40. Daydreaming
_____	_____	41. Feeling the presence of the Lord in my life, praying, or worshipping
_____	_____	42. Smelling a flower
_____	_____	43. Talking about old times or special interests
_____	_____	44. Going to auctions or garage sales
_____	_____	45. Traveling
_____	_____	46. Other: _____

2. Next, place a check in column 2 if you've done the event in the last thirty days.

3. Circle the number next to the events that you'd probably enjoy doing (on a good day).

4. Compare the first and second columns. Notice if there are many items that you've enjoyed in the past but currently are not doing very often.

5. Using the completed pleasant events schedule for ideas, make a list of the twenty-five activities that you feel you'd enjoy doing the most.

6. Make a plan to do more pleasant activities. Start with the simplest ones you are most likely to enjoy. Do as many pleasant events as you reasonably can. Try to do at least one each day, perhaps more on weekends. Write your plan on a calendar, and carry out this written plan for at least two weeks. Each time you do an activity, rate it on a scale of 1 to 5 for pleasure (5 being highly enjoyable). Doing so tests the stress-induced distortion that nothing is enjoyable. This rating may also help you later replace less enjoyable activities with others.

   Please note: If you are depressed, it is common to find that your old favorite activities are now the most difficult to enjoy, particularly if you tried them when you were very low and failed to enjoy them. You might say, "I can't even enjoy my favorite activity," which makes you feel even more depressed. These events will become pleasant again as depression lifts. For now, start with other, simple activities. Gradually try your old favorites as your mood lifts.

Some Tips About Pleasure

- Tune into the physical world. Pay less attention to your thoughts. Feel the wind, or the soap suds as you wash the car. See and hear.

- Before doing an event, set yourself up to enjoy it. Identify three things you will enjoy about it. For example, say, "I will enjoy the sunshine. I will enjoy the breeze. I will enjoy talking with my brother Will." Relax, and imagine yourself enjoying each aspect of the event as you repeat each statement.

- Ask yourself, "What will I do to make the activity enjoyable?"

- If you are concerned that you might not enjoy an activity that you'd like to try, break it up into steps. Think small, so that you can be satisfied in reaching your goal. For example, if you want to clean your entire house, start by only cleaning the house for ten minutes, then stop. Reward yourself with a "Good job!" pat on the back.

- Check your schedule for balance. Can you spread out the "need tos" to make room for some "want tos"?

- Time is limited, so use it wisely. You needn't do activities you don't like just because they're convenient.

Little Things That Make Life Worth Living

By Mark Patinkin, newspaper columnist with the *Providence Journal-Bulletin*

I recently wrote a column on little things that drive me nuts, like vanity plates, two-pound yippy dogs, and sticky floors in movie theaters. Afterward, a few less cynical types urged me to give equal time to the other side. So today, a second list:

- The smell of burning leaves in autumn.

- A hot shower when you're freezing.

- Pizza delivered to your door.

- Being the first in a crowded supermarket to notice a cashier announcing a newly opened register.

- Automatic icemakers.

- The one morning every six months that your three-year-old actually sleeps to 7:30 a.m.

- The service department saying, "No problem. That's on warranty."

- Hearing the phone ring just as you're sitting down to dinner, then realizing you have the answering machine on.

- Terry cloth bathrobes.

- That combined smell of…new-mown grass…and popcorn that hits you when you walk into a baseball stadium.

- Dogs that sense when you're sad and come over to make you feel better.

- Room service.

- Those two weeks in spring when even the drabbest shrubs are in full Technicolor.

- Having nothing scheduled Sunday morning except reading the newspaper.

- Learning at O'Hare Airport that your plane is at gate 1 rather than 322.

- Heated pools.

- Cruising down the highway while the opposite lanes are in a five-mile traffic jam.

- The crack of a hard ball against a wood bat.

- The zoo on a sunny day.

- A full moon just above the horizon at 7:30 p.m. when it looks the size of a dinner plate.

- A parking space four steps from the restaurant door.

- Photo finishing in minutes.

- Deciding you've had it with the world, then checking your calendar and realizing you have nothing booked for the next five nights.

- Geese flying overhead shaped in a perfect "V."

- Lying on the grass in the countryside staring up at the brightest stars you've ever seen.

- Microwave popcorn.

- The airline ticket clerk explaining that they sold too many coach tickets and will be bumping you to first class.

- Eating a hot dog with a live baseball game in front of it.

- Blood-red autumn leaves.

- A cool breeze on a hot day.

- Your suitcase being the first one to appear on the airport baggage carousel.

(Author note: If you enjoyed this reminder to appreciate life's loveliness, then you will probably also enjoy Barbara Ann Kipfer's *14,000 Things to Be Happy About*, 1990.)

CHAPTER 33

Prepare for Setbacks

You have now acquired a substantial number of skills to build self-esteem. Regardless of how secure one's self-esteem, there is still the possibility that it can be "blown away" by a salient "failure" or unfortunate event. So it is imperative to develop skills for riding out "failures"—for keeping self-esteem strong and secure during the storms of life that will inevitably come. In some ways, the flop inoculation exercise below is a review of the skills you've learned. Before we start, let's first preassess what you understand "failure" to be.

1. What are things people (including yourself) fail at?

2. What does "failure" mean?

3. What has helped you to cope with "failure" during, before, and after?

What are things people "fail" at? Here are a few possible answers:

- Jobs

- Marriages

- Parenting

- School

- Reaching ideal weight

- Smoking cessation

- Keeping moral standards

- Making time for fun

- Reaching goals

Did you think of others?

What does "failure" mean? Here are some possible answers:

- Nobody loves me

- Rejection

- I'm no good

- Not maintaining my self-esteem

- I'm human

What has helped you to cope with "failure" in the past? Some have mentioned talking it over, giving oneself permission to fail, forgiving oneself, realizing that it won't matter much years from now, and changing course.

Are you getting the idea that people vary greatly in how they view failure and in their abilities to cope with it?

Approaching Perfection

Let's take a look at "failure" in a way that expands some of the concepts previously explored.

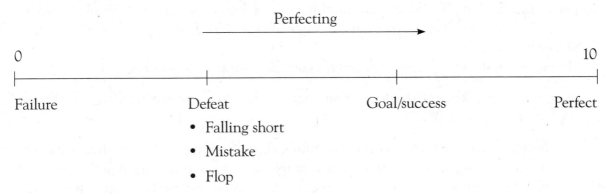

"Perfect" means completed, finished, and without defect or flaw. Since humans are fallible, we can only approach perfection. "Goal" or "success" refers to attaining something we want, be it for happiness, comfort, or growth. Because humans are always in the process of becoming their best selves, a "goal" or a "success" is placed somewhat to the left of "perfect." You might argue that you can set a goal to save 5 percent of your income and meet that goal perfectly. But aside from quantifiable endeavors such as that, goals are generally imperfectly met. That is, improvements can ideally be made no matter how well one performs. "Perfecting" means making oneself more nearly perfect. It can occur as one attempts to reach a goal or after one has met a goal.

People imprecisely say, "I'm a failure" (which means "I always and in every way fail"), when they mean to say, "I failed to reach my goal" or "I fell short of my goal" or "I made a mistake." To slightly alter Hubert H. Humphrey's famous quotation to improve our understanding: "There's a big difference between failure and defeat. Failure is when you are defeated and [never] learn nor contribute anything."

Handling Flops

Rather than using the label "failure" to refer to unfortunate events or behaviors, falling short, mistakes, and so forth, I prefer using the word "flop." "Flop" sounds less serious and less permanent than failure, and it refers to an external, not the core.

One more concept is worth reiterating before moving to the skill-building activity. Research demonstrates that a pessimistic thinking style held by men in their twenties predicts poor physical health when those men reach their forties and fifties (Peterson, Seligman, and Vaillant 1988). When an unfortunate event occurred, the pessimistic men tended to fully fault themselves, believe that they would never improve, and believe that misfortune would spill over into all areas of life. For example, after failing a math test, a pessimist might think, "It's me—I'm a failure. I always mess up on math tests. I just am unlucky when things really matter." Optimists, on the other hand—whose physical health fared better years later—might think, "I wasn't up to par physically that day. It's a one-time thing, and it won't ruin my life." Similar thinking styles tend to distinguish drug addicts who relapse after slipping from those who rebound from similar setbacks.

From such research, we can form certain guidelines for handling setbacks:

1. Admit mistakes. Don't deny responsibility; rather, focus on remedial action—that is, what you need to *do*.

2. Reframe the event. Instead of condemning the self, which erodes self-esteem and saps motivation, focus on externals. For example, instead of thinking, *What's wrong with me?* (The answer is easy: we're imperfect!), focus on externals (fatigue, incomplete preparation, too little experience, and so forth).

Instead of considering something a total failure, remind yourself that there will probably be other opportunities. After experiencing a "flop," ask yourself the following questions:

- Did certain things go well?

- What are the advantages of not getting what I wanted?

- What coping skills could I learn from this?

- Were there signs of an impending crisis that I did not heed?

- If a similar event occurs again, what could I do to attend to such signs earlier?

Flop Inoculation: An Exercise

Guidelines, such as those discussed above, can be helpful. Let's put them into practice now. The following exercise derives from stress inoculation, a strategy developed by psychologist Donald Meichenbaum (1985). He posits that people can prepare for stress by practicing what they will think and do before, during, and after a stressful event. Exposure to small and safe doses of imaginary stress can "inoculate" us, just as a small injection can inoculate us against disease. In the exercise below, the stressful event is the prospect of "flopping" (for example, falling short of a goal, making a mistake, performing poorly, or forgetting to use self-esteem skills when criticized).

Step 1: Put a check by any statements that have meaning for you as part of your coping repertoire relative to mistakes and setbacks.

Before

- [ ] It will be fun to succeed, but it won't be the end of the world if I don't.

- [ ] I'm new at this, so I'll be a little more careful until I get the hang of it.

- [ ] I see this as a new challenge, not a problem or a threat.

- [ ] This is a gift (opportunity, adventure, or challenge), not a problem.

- [ ] I'll approach this with curiosity, not fear or self-doubt.

- [ ] I'll aim to do a good job. I won't ruin the experience with perfectionism.

- [ ] I have as much right as anyone to try my hand at this.

- [ ] I'll look for success in little steps and ways. I'll dismiss all-or-nothing demands of myself.

- [ ] I am embarking without absolute certainty of all the facts and outcomes, and that's okay.

- [ ] I have the right to decide what's best for me and to implement my decisions with confidence and without apology.

- [ ] I calmly examine the probable outcomes of my actions.

- [ ] If I'm not uptight about mistakes, I'll also be more creative.

- [ ] My focus is development, not mistakes.

- [ ] It's okay to try and to "flop."

- [ ] I'll choose the course that seems best.

- [ ] I'll relax and consider different approaches and their probable consequences. Then I'll make the best choice I can.

- [ ] I'm optimistic and open to all possibilities.

- [ ] What will this challenge require of me? What can I realistically give?

- [ ] I don't have to be perfect to do well.

- [ ] It could be fun to try and stretch in the process.

- [ ] I'm not afraid to risk and fall short because my worth comes from within.

- [ ] What's the worst that could happen?

During

- [ ] This is difficult. Relax and focus on the task.

- [ ] Take it step-by-step. Feel good about little successes.

- [ ] It's too bad things aren't perfect, but they're not a catastrophe.

- [ ] Everyone makes mistakes and has rough edges. Why should I assume I don't?

- [ ] My quest to transcend and shape these imperfections is important.

- [ ] Relax and enjoy the process, glitches and all.

- [ ] I'm not a deity. I'm human. It's okay to be imperfect. I'll do my best.

- [ ] I'll focus on the process. The outcome will take care of itself.

- [ ] I'll take it one step at a time.

- [ ] Remember humor. It reminds me I'm neither as great as I wish I were nor as bad as a lot of people might think I am.

- [ ] This informs me about my present limitations.

After

- [ ] I had a weakness. That was then. This is now.

- [ ] I'm just a beginner at this, and beginners have to expect mistakes now and then.

- [ ] This isn't a signpost to the rest of my life.

- [ ] I am hopeful.

- [ ] I take responsibility for understanding the situation, but I'll not necessarily take the blame, nor will I ever condemn myself.

- [ ] My judgment and behavior were bad, but *I* am not bad.

- [ ] Okay, now what? What are my options now?

- [ ] This revealed a weakness. This is part of me, not all of me.

- [ ] The weak parts are rough edges. At the core I am worthwhile.

- [ ] I love myself for this.

- [ ] I am still here for myself, to be a friend through this period.

☐ I have the courage to love myself when I'm imperfect (this is my foundation for growth).

☐ No matter what happened, I am still worthwhile, precious, and unique.

☐ I admit that sometimes I'm this way. It disappoints me. I can do something about it.

☐ I accept the way I sometimes am, and I love those imperfect parts of me, too. This love gives me the security to grow in those areas.

☐ No matter how bad it seemed, certain things went okay. I've gained wisdom and experience.

☐ I'll change my course so I can be happier.

☐ I am teachable. I can change and grow.

☐ I can shape my future.

☐ I can use experiences from the past and convert them to strengths.

☐ I have the right to improve and develop each day.

☐ I have the right to make mistakes. I am adequate enough to admit to them and to repair them as much as humanly possible.

☐ This will pass.

☐ This will help me be better, wiser, and stronger.

☐ I have the right to correct my course.

☐ This mistake is a way to look at what I'm doing and to see what I want to correct.

☐ This is not really a failure, but efforts toward success. (Inspired by Babe Ruth)

☐ Instead of "failure," think bad choice, bad judgment, missteps, false start, momentary loss of my way, a blip, or falling short.

☐ I'm adequate enough to learn from this and to improve next time.

☐ Mistakes show me what I want to improve and correct and what's not working.

☐ I'll be wiser next time.

☐ Mistakes make me human and fallible, just like everyone else.

☐ Okay, I botched that; if at first you don't succeed…

☐ Okay, so I mess up 10 percent of the time. The rest of the time I do pretty well.

- [ ] There's a bright side to this even if I don't see it yet.

- [ ] Isn't it great that I can do such a ridiculous thing and still have hope?

- [ ] Isn't it interesting that I sometimes condemn myself overall for a weakness or imperfection?

- [ ] I made a mistake. I am not a mistake.

- [ ] I am more than my mistake. There is more to my life history than this.

- [ ] I erred; now I'm returning right away to my good patterns.

- [ ] I did it before. I'll do it again.

- [ ] I believe things will improve.

- [ ] Okay, I handled this. I can handle other challenges, too.

- [ ] This is not the end of the world.

- [ ] My downfall isn't the end of me.

- [ ] The sun will come up tomorrow.

- [ ] No use crying over spilled milk. It's water under the bridge.

- [ ] No one is a "failure" until he gives up altogether.

- [ ] I'll not be defeated twice: once by circumstances and once by myself. (Inspired by Lowell Bennion)

- [ ] Eventually I'll improve. There will be another chance.

- [ ] This was a difficult and complex task. It was made more difficult by my inexperience (lack of guidance or help, noise, weather, temperature, interruptions, my not feeling up to it, or other difficult circumstances).

- [ ] What will I learn for the next time?

- [ ] I can't possibly control everything.

- [ ] "Failure is an event, never a person." (Dr. William D. Brown)

- [ ] "Oh, boy! Now I'm really going to learn something." (Harold "Doc" Edgerton)

- [ ] Failure isn't final. Start again.

- [ ] Years from now, will anyone really care about this?

Step 2: Below, write fifteen statements you would most like to remember to tell yourself before, during, and after the times when your behavior falls short of your goals. The statements need not come from the above lists.

"Before" Statements

1.

2.

3.

4.

5.

"During" Statements

1.

2.

3.

4.

5.

"After" Statements

1.

2.

3.

4.

5.

During each of the next three days, select an event with "flop potential." Spend fifteen minutes mentally rehearsing what you will think before, during, and after the "flop."

For a most amusing and profound treatment of realistic optimism and dealing with failure, read Dr. Seuss's *Oh, the Places You'll Go!* (1990).

CHAPTER 34

An Overview of Growing

In this section we have explored important ideas and skills regarding the third building block of self-esteem, growing. Let's review the key points and skills that you have learned and practiced.

Active Ideas

1. Growing is an ongoing process that is never fully completed.

2. The growth process is a way of loving. It is satisfying because it starts from the secure inner base of worth and love.

3. At an emotional level, the process says, "I'm glad inside and unafraid to be growing—becoming even better."

4. Ascent is difficult. Expect hard work.

5. Growing is not competitive or comparative. You can select your course and pace. As with weight plans and exercise, it is wise to pick a pace that you can maintain throughout life.

6. Growing means elevating others along with the self.

7. Growing results from applying principles and pleasures that elevate.

8. Because growing is like climbing the staircase, and not just arriving at a certain place, you need not arrive to experience self-esteem. You need only to know in your heart that you're on track and moving ahead.

Acquired Skills

1. *Even though I'm not perfect…nevertheless*

2. Just for the fun of it (contemplating possibilities)

3. The loving, fearless, searching, and honest moral inventory

4. Forgiving yourself and others

5. Scheduling pleasant activities

6. Flop inoculation

To reinforce these important ideas and skills, please take a few moments to respond to the following questions. You might first wish to flip back through the preceding pages of this section to review what you've done.

1. Which of the ideas have had the most meaning to you?

2. Which skills do you most wish to return to and use again?

3. What do you need right now? Are there skills in this section that you would like to spend more time with? If so, take the time to do so.

Summing Up

Each person has been created miraculously, in so many ways. It is important to quietly recognize and appreciate this so that you may grow with satisfaction and joy.

Don't let mistakes define you. Don't let criticism, falling short of goals, past traumas, lack of money or status, or any other externals define you. Each person is too precious and complex to be so narrowly defined.

In our journey together we have explored a variety of self-esteem-building skills. As with any other skills, self-esteem skills take time to acquire and practice to maintain. Perhaps you will incorporate some of these skills into your life without much conscious thought. Perhaps other skills will require that you deliberately set aside time to practice.

Do not hesitate to go back from time to time to repeat each of these valuable skills. If life throws you a curve that sets your self-esteem back somewhat, remember to again refer to this book and to rehearse the skills that have had meaning for you. If self-esteem can be built once, it can be built up again.

Like any other important health practice, self-esteem building and maintenance are parts of an ongoing process. However, like other useful habits, self-esteem skills, once acquired, become almost second nature and, therefore, easier to apply.

To summarize, and to reinforce your most important skills, please review the entire book and list below those ideas and skills that you most want to remember. These lists will also serve as quick reminders during difficult times.

Ideas You Want to Remember

Skills You Want to Remember

Acknowledgments

No one sees clearly without standing on the shoulders of those who have preceded us.

I'd like to first thank the late Morris Rosenberg, professor of sociology, University of Maryland. Dr. Rosenberg's theorizing, meticulous research, and teaching have stimulated my own thinking on self-esteem immeasurably. Similarly, I am grateful to the late Dr. Stanley Coopersmith, whose germinal research combined with Dr. Rosenberg's provide the theoretical foundations of this book.

Special thanks go to Claudia Howard, whose patient dialogue, theoretical insights, and practical ideas lifted my thinking far beyond where it would have gone otherwise.

Thanks to Dr. John Burt, former dean of the College of Health and Human Performance, who taught me to make thinking a hobby. Teaming with him in teaching his Ways of Knowing about Human Stress and Tension course allowed me to first wrestle with turning theory regarding stress and self-esteem into practice.

And thanks to the students of the University of Maryland, some older, some younger, who have helped me to sharpen the theory and practice of teaching self-esteem.

I express gratitude to the cognitive theorists and practitioners who influenced chapter 5. Albert Ellis originated the ABC model, catastrophizing, and shoulds. Aaron Beck originated the term "automatic thoughts"; the term "distortions"; most of the distortions presently used in cognitive therapy; the idea of basic (core) beliefs; and the idea of recording thoughts, distortions, and moods. David Burns wrote *Feeling Good*, a very useful application of Beck's theories. With great gratitude, I also acknowledge those who inspired chapter 15, including Russell M. Nelson (*The Power Within Us*), L. Schlossberg and G. D. Zuidema (*The Johns Hopkins Atlas of Human Functional Anatomy*), the National Geographic Society (*The Incredible Machine*), and J. D. Ratcliff (the *I Am Joe's...*series).

Other pioneering researchers and practitioners have added immeasurably to this edition. I am thankful to Drs. Kristin Neff, Sharon Salzberg, James W. Pennebaker, and Robert D. Enright for their thoughtful efforts regarding self-compassion, loving-kindness, expressive writing, and forgiving, respectively.

I am particularly appreciative of Bev Monis, who produced this manuscript with saintly patience, and Carol Jackson, who created the beautiful graphics for the original edition, and upon which this edition's graphics were based.

Finally, I wish to acknowledge with sincere gratitude all the wonderful, conscientious, and encouraging people at New Harbinger Publications, especially Patrick Fanning, Jueli Gastwirth, Kasey Pfaff, Amy Shoup, and Michele Waters.

Appendices

Guidelines for Helping the Person in Distress

The following model depicts both how a person can reduce stress symptoms and the relationship of self-esteem to the restoration of good health.

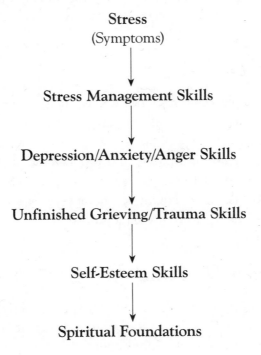

Stress
(Symptoms)

↓

Stress Management Skills

↓

Depression/Anxiety/Anger Skills

↓

Unfinished Grieving/Trauma Skills

↓

Self-Esteem Skills

↓

Spiritual Foundations

Managing Stress

"Stress" is a rather general term. The person experiencing stress might manifest symptoms ranging from simple tension to headaches, fatigue, agitation, difficulty concentrating, insomnia, mood disturbance, worry, and/or illnesses ranging from high blood pressure to PMS.

Underlying medical causes must first be ruled out or treated. Common medical causes include sleep apnea, thyroid disorders, gum disease, elevated cholesterol, and diabetes. Substances that increase stress symptoms are best avoided or minimized. These include nicotine (which greatly increases depression and anxiety symptoms), excessive caffeine or alcohol, recreational drugs, and certain medications, such as anticholinergic drugs and stimulants. Anticholinergic drugs include antihistamines, tranquilizers, sleeping pills, and tricyclic antidepressants. Discuss with your doctor ways to minimize these medications or replace them with other medications or nondrug treatments.

Stress symptoms can then often be reduced with traditional stress management skills, including systematic relaxation training (such as progressive muscular relaxation, meditation, autogenic methods, abdominal breathing, or imagery), time management, communication skills, sleep hygiene, exercise and dietary adjustments, yoga, and other coping strategies. Such strategies are quite useful for nearly all people. If they are not sufficiently effective, then helpers might look for underlying depression, anxiety, or excessive anger.

Depression, Anxiety, Anger

Clinical depression, for example, often responds well to the skills learned in cognitive therapy, or a combination of cognitive therapy and antidepressant medications, once medical causes have been ruled out or treated.

Any combination of depression, anxiety, and problematic anger can lead to a range of medical illnesses, so it is important to treat these conditions. These are typically treated with here-and-now coping skills (such as cognitive therapy or writing about present worries). Traditional stress management skills are useful adjuncts.

Unresolved Grief or Trauma

If the above approaches are not completely effective, or underlying issues are uncovered, helpers would then address unfinished grief and trauma issues. It is estimated that at least 15 to 20 percent of people who seek professional counseling for clinical depression or anxiety have at the root of those symptoms unresolved grief or trauma. Unresolved grief and trauma can result from a range of events, including the death of a child or parent, physical or sexual abuse, parental abandonment, amputation, accidents, crime, war, civil unrest, rape, or job loss (Worden 1982). We now understand that adverse childhood experiences that are not resolved can result in a range of psychological, medical, and functional problems in adulthood. Symptoms can include emotional numbing, depression, anxiety, anger, hyperactivity, physical stress, intrusive thoughts or nightmares, insomnia, deliberate self-injury, and dissociation. All trauma involves loss, whether it is loss of innocence or loss of a limb. Worden has identified several active tasks that help people complete the grieving and healing process and move on. Since the Vietnam War, we have learned a wide range of very effective ways to help trauma survivors settle haunting memories and heal. *The Post-Traumatic Stress Disorder Sourcebook* offers an overview of treatment options. Trauma treatments are very effective but require specialized training. The Sidran Traumatic Stress Institute can help locate a trauma specialist in your area. (Both are listed in the "Recommended Resources" section.) Traditional stress management skills are very helpful but usually not sufficient for the treatment of grief and trauma issues.

Restoring Self-Esteem

Typically, damaged self-esteem must be restored before a person will feel whole again. For example, the survivor of sexual abuse usually needs to feel a sense of self-worth again before he or she can release bitterness and the desire for revenge. The person who is chronically angry and defensive will find it easier to withstand criticism once inner security is developed. Damaged self-esteem can be both a risk factor and a result of symptoms. For example, self-dislike can predispose one to depression. Since depression often impairs performance, depression tends to increase self-dislike. In either case, developing self-esteem will often help reduce symptoms and aid recovery. If trauma has damaged self-esteem (for example, a rape victim feels like a worthless object), healing from the trauma might be necessary before self-esteem skills can be effectively learned and applied.

The Strength of a Spiritual Foundation

Spiritual foundations and skills can help reduce symptoms at all levels of the model illustrated above. For example, one who understands infinite, divine love might find it easier to love and forgive the self and others. Respect and regard for all humans might help one understand unconditional human worth. Peace of conscience, forgiveness, and an eternal perspective can help reduce stress, worries, anxiety, and depression. Spirituality and religious practice have been linked to improved mental and physical well-being in numerous studies.

Additional Comments

- While a skilled professional can facilitate the reduction of symptoms, the ultimate goal is self-reliance: that the suffering individual will learn the skills that can help prevent the recurrence of symptoms, reduce their severity if they do recur, and eventually return the person to optimal health.

- The helping model is not a rigid model but a flexible one. For example, if it is obvious that a person's symptoms are due to severe clinical depression, then the mental health professional would probably not initially use traditional stress management strategies. Rather, more aggressive approaches to rapidly reduce symptoms would be tried, such as antidepressant medication or electroconvulsive therapy. Cognitive behavioral psychotherapy and stress management skills could then be introduced. If a trauma history identified unresolved trauma and a diagnosis of post-traumatic stress disorder (PTSD) was made, then treating PTSD would be the first priority.

- Although spiritual and religious practices have been found to facilitate recovery from trauma, trauma can numb feelings, including spiritual feelings. Treating and healing traumatic wounds can sometimes help one open up again to spiritual feelings.

- Self-esteem is sometimes called the common denominator because it underlies so many stress symptoms. Whether low self-esteem is a cause or a result of symptoms, self-esteem skills will often be useful to reduce those symptoms. However, these skills do not eliminate the need for a balanced, comprehensive treatment plan that utilizes all necessary approaches.

APPENDIX II

Forgiving the Self

Almost all cultures have values as to what constitutes right and wrong behavior. In religion, "sin" refers to behaviors that violate such standards. "Guilt" is the feeling that alerts one to the wrongness of certain behaviors and motivates one to avoid them. This appendix focuses on "healthy guilt," which implies that standards are reasonable and individuals assume appropriate responsibility for their own behavior—no more, no less. The denial of the feeling of healthy guilt has deleterious consequences, just as denial of any feeling does. "Shame," as it is often used in contemporary psychology, refers to the unhealthy perception that one is bad to the core.

"Repentance" implies a return to a former state. Among theologians, there is general agreement as to the steps of repentance, which returns one to a cleansed state characterized by, among other things, God's forgiveness:

1. Acknowledge that you committed the behavior and that the behavior was wrong.

2. Acknowledge that you hurt the self and others, if others were hurt by the behavior. It is constructive to feel hurt, sadness, disappointment, and empathy and to fully realize the connection between these feelings and the behavior that led to them.

3. Confess to God (and others who might have been affected by the behavior) an awareness of the wrong and the consequences of the behavior and appropriate sorrow for the damage.

4. Make amends when possible (for example, if something was taken, replace it; if another's feelings were hurt or self-esteem was damaged, apologize).

5. Forsake the behavior (that is, determine to not repeat it and take the steps necessary to ensure it does not recur).

6. Commit to holy living. "Holy" derives from the same root as "health," and it implies wholeness, integration, and no divisions between values and behaviors.

After completing the repentance process, some may still find it difficult to forgive the self. So the following ideas might help.

Wrong behaviors are externals. They surround the core and, like a dirty film on the surface of a body of water, might prevent light from entering or leaving. One might *feel*, therefore, like one is dark and worthless to the core. However, this is a feeling that does not reflect reality. Make sure you interpret the feeling correctly. The sad feeling is a commentary on a behavior that needs to be altered, not your core value! Resist all impulses to interpret the sad feeling as a commentary of worthlessness. When repentance has occurred, one breaks free from the behavior and can more accurately experience core worth again.

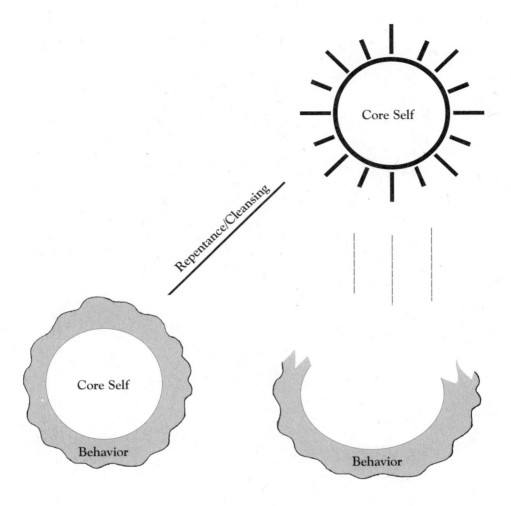

The behavior may be remembered, but the pain subsides.

As World War II concentration camp survivor Victor Frankl (1978) wrote, "It is a human prerogative to become guilty and it is a human responsibility to overcome guilt." We ask ourselves: How much is left? What can I actively do to embrace responsibility? To improve? To render the past, present, and future meaningful?

Touching the Past with Love

Every living soul has experienced painful events. Perhaps some of these events still hurt and prevent you from fully experiencing self-esteem. The skill that follows helps one to heal and strengthen emotionally, and to release the painful emotions so that one can move on. The primary agent of healing is love.

This exercise is optional: some have a great desire to neutralize the pain of past events and benefit greatly from doing so, others have no desire to revisit the past, and yet others would prefer to revisit the past with the help of a mental health professional.

Directions

1. Find a quiet place where you can remain undisturbed for about thirty minutes.

2. Identify an event in your life that is still painful. Such difficult moments might include times when

    - people hurt or shamed you (for example, with unkind words, criticism, abuse, bullying, or taunts);

    - you felt alone, neglected, rejected, or abandoned; or

    - you were disappointed in your own behavior or performance (for example, you were overwhelmed and did not know how to cope, or your behavior was wrong from an ethical standpoint).

3. Name the person who experienced this difficult time your younger self.

4. Name your present self—who possesses greater experience, wisdom, and love—the wiser self.

5. Imagine that you, the wiser self, travel back in time to the difficult event, and you approach your younger self. Your younger self looks up and sees you. Your eyes meet and there is an affinity and trust; your younger self is willing to listen to you.

6. You enter into a dialogue with your younger self. You ask the younger self, "What is troubling you?" The younger self expresses the facts and feelings of the event. You listen with great empathy and understanding.

7. You ask, "What would help?" You listen intently with your ears and your heart for what is expressed verbally and silently. You perceive and provide for your younger self's needs, such as the need for:

- Empathy, which says, in effect, "I understand; you are not alone."

- Instruction. Perhaps you can teach skills that you recently learned, such as the *nevertheless* skill.

- Support and encouragement. For example, "Considering your experience and training, you're doing well!"; "It will get better!"; "You'll make it through this. I know that you will."

- Physical help or protection. For example, you might imagine stepping between the younger self and a bully or an abuser.

- Advice. Think together. Use the experiences and wisdom of both selves to brainstorm solutions:

  - Perhaps you could advise the child who was abused to say, "That's no way to treat a child." The wiser self stands alongside the child offering protection and support.

  - The adult might say to a critical supervisor, "I see your point. I'd like you to help me. I think I'll develop faster if you point out the positives, too."

  - If the younger self behaved in a way that was wrong or unethical, you might explore together the principles and behaviors that favor human growth. Imagine reminding the younger self about these wiser principles and behaviors. Imagine guiding the younger self in applying these behaviors. Then see the younger self actually doing them and any other helpful behaviors, such as apologizing, expressing sorrow for hurt that the behavior caused, making amends, or expressing kindness. Allow the younger self to experience the more peaceful feelings of the new behaviors and to share with your present self what that is like. Provide assurance that this is the wiser course.

- Love. This is most important! Love might be communicated through

  - a loving, gentle, accepting look, in which eyes meet eyes;

  - loving words (for example, "I love you");

  - a hug or embrace; and

  - a soothing touch.

8. Tell your younger self that you are returning "back to the future" and that your love will remain with the younger self.

9. Let your attention return to the present. Use a *nevertheless*-like statement, such as "That *was* a difficult time, *nevertheless* I love me." Allow the healing feeling of love to sink in and surround you.

Repeat this exercise for a total of four days, using a different difficult event for each day. To reinforce this exercise, I recommend that you record each experience in writing. Writing helps put the past in perspective and provides distance. It also seems to sharpen and reinforce solutions.

You might notice a drop in mood during the days that you practice this exercise. Thereafter, mood typically rises above the point where it existed before you began using the exercise. This process might be likened to lancing a boil: some pain must be experienced in order to facilitate healing.

I once had a student who remembered that when she was a child, her mother often spoke very critically about the child's father. One day, as a young child, the student said something critical about her father in a department store, and her mother shook her violently and screamed, "Don't talk about your father that way!" As an adult, the student still remembered how shocked and hurt she felt, and she selected this event to work with in the exercise described above.

During the exercise, the wiser self coached the child to ask her mother, "Why is it that you yelled at me when I said what you had taught me to say?" The wiser self protected the child but then noticed the pain in the mother's eyes. So she hugged the mother. Then the wiser self told the child that she would miss out if she came back to the present with her. She gave the child a stone as a symbol of comfort and of the love the wiser self felt for her.

The Insights of Imagery

Imagery, such as imagining your present self communicating with a younger self, can yield surprising insights and solutions to difficult past moments. The example above, of a woman communicating with her mother through a younger version of herself, is an excellent example of reworking a past event and then surrounding the pain with love.

If you chose to participate in this four-day exercise, then please complete the following at the end of the four days:

1. Spend one day reviewing the principles and skills that you have learned thus far.

2. Spend three days applying the skills that you found to be most meaningful.

These steps help to lift the mood and return the focus to the present.

Recommended Resources

Self-Esteem and Unconditional Love

Petrie, A., and J. Petrie. 1986. *Mother Teresa*. Petrie Productions, DVD. A powerful documentary with universal messages of unconditional love, forgiveness, and faith.

Schiraldi, G. R. 2007. *Ten Simple Solutions for Building Self-Esteem*. Oakland, CA: New Harbinger. Combines mindfulness, acceptance and commitment therapy, and traditional psychological strategies for raising self-esteem.

Seuss, Dr. 1990. *Oh, the Places You'll Go!* New York: Random House. A clever, humorous treatise on human growth and fallibility. Powerful messages for people of all ages.

Heart Coherence

The HeartMath Institute in Boulder Creek, California (800-711-6221, http://www.heartmath .org, http://www.store.heartmath.com) is a great resource for books, videos, music, and affordable technology that enables one to monitor heart rhythms in real time as one practices HeartMath skills. Seeing your heart coherence increase can be very motivating.

The following are very useful books about heart coherence:

Childre, D., and D. Rozman. 2003. *Transforming Anger: The HeartMath Solution for Letting Go of Rage, Frustration, and Irritation*. Oakland, CA: New Harbinger.

Childre, D., and D. Rozman. 2005. *Transforming Stress: The HeartMath Solution for Relieving Worry, Fatigue, and Tension*. Oakland, CA: New Harbinger.

Self-Compassion

Neff, K. 2011. *Self-Compassion: The Proven Power of Being Kind to Yourself*. New York: William Morrow. Learn how to replace harsh self-criticism and judgment with kindness. If you are going to obtain one book on self-compassion, this is the one. *The Mindful Path to Self-Compassion* (2009), written by Dr. Christopher Germer, is also very useful. Dr. Neff's wonderful website, http://www.self-compassion.org, also offers excellent self-compassion scales, exercises, and meditations.

Salzberg, S. 1995. *Loving-Kindness: The Revolutionary Art of Happiness*. Boston: Shambhala. Excellent overview of loving-kindness meditation, which complements self-compassion and has been found to improve mental health.

Journal Writing

Pennebaker, J. W. 1997. *Opening Up: The Healing Power of Expressing Emotion*. New York: Guilford Press. This is Dr. Pennebaker's first book—a classic.

Pennebaker, J. W., and J. F. Evans. 2014. *Expressive Writing: Words That Heal*. Enumclaw, WA: Idyll Arbor, Inc. Explains why verbalizing emotional pain from childhood or adult experiences reduces distress. Includes many ideas on how to make journal writing effective.

Forgiving

Enright, R. D. 2001. *Forgiveness Is a Choice: A Step-by-Step Process for Resolving Anger and Restoring Hope*. Washington, DC: American Psychological Association. Well worth the read.

Enright, R. D. 2012. *The Forgiving Life: A Pathway to Overcoming Resentment and Creating a Legacy of Love*. Washington, DC: American Psychological Association. The foremost forgiveness researcher describes forgiveness as an often difficult process that releases resentment; fills the void with compassion for both the wounder and the wounded; and blesses the forgiver, our families and associates, and sometimes the offender. Many rich and practical steps.

Trauma

Schiraldi, G. R. 2016. *The Post-Traumatic Stress Disorder Sourcebook*. New York: McGraw-Hill. Exposure to traumatic events, such as sexual abuse, rape, terrorism, and war, can damage self-esteem. This book clearly explains and normalizes the bewildering symptoms of PTSD and describes the rich range of effective healing options and resources.

The Sidran Traumatic Stress Institute in Baltimore, Maryland (410-825-8888; http://www.sidran.org) can help you locate psychotherapists specializing in PTSD and offers readings and other resources.

Resilience

Resilience Training International (www.ResilienceFirst.com) provides skills-based resilience training to prevent stress-related conditions, to facilitate recovery, and to optimize health and performance. Resilience and self-esteem are highly correlated. Dr. Glenn Schiraldi founded and owns the organization.

Happiness

Happiness and self-esteem are highly correlated around the world. These are my two favorite happiness books:

Brooks, A. C. 2008. *Gross National Happiness: Why Happiness Matters for America—and How We Can Get More of It.* New York: Basic. An accomplished researcher uses large and reputable databases, mostly from recent studies, to draw conclusions on topics—including politics, family, and religious values—as they relate to happiness.

Lyubomirsky, S. 2008. *The How of Happiness: A Scientific Approach to Getting the Life You Want.* New York: Penguin. A masterful combination of solid research and practical, tested methods to enhance happiness.

Scholarly Classics

Those interested in early scholarly works about the causes and consequences of various levels of self-esteem may refer to these titles:

Coopersmith, S. 1967. *The Antecedents of Self-Esteem.* San Francisco: Freeman.

Rosenberg, M. 1965. *Society and the Adolescent Self-Image.* Princeton, NJ: Princeton University Press.

Bibliography

Alexander, F. G. 1932. *The Medical Value of Psychoanalysis*. New York: Norton.

Borkovec, T. D., L. Wilkinson, R. Folensbee, and C. Lerman. 1983. "Stimulus Control Applications to the Treatment of Worry." *Behavior Research and Therapy* 21: 247–50.

Bourne, R. A., Jr. 1992. "Rational Responses to Four of Ellis' Irrational Beliefs." Unpublished class handout presented by the Upledger Institute, Palm Beach Gardens, FL.

Bradshaw, J. 1988. *Healing the Shame That Binds You*. Deerfield Beach, FL: Health Communications, Inc.

Briggs, D. C. 1977. *Celebrate Yourself: Making Life Work for You*. Garden City, NY: Doubleday.

Brothers, J. 1990. "What Really Makes Men and Women Attractive." *Parade*, August 5.

Brown, S. L., and G. R. Schiraldi. 2000. "Reducing Symptoms of Anxiety and Depression: Combined Results of a Cognitive-Behavioral College Course." Paper presented at Anxiety Disorders Association of America National Conference, Washington, DC, March 24.

Burns, D. 1980. "The Perfectionist's Script for Self-Defeat." *Psychology Today*, November, 34–51.

Burns, G. 1984. *Dr. Burns' Prescription for Happiness*. New York: G. P. Putnam's Sons.

Canfield, J. 1985. "Body Appreciation." In *Wisdom, Purpose, and Love*. Santa Barbara, CA: Self-Esteem Seminars/Chicken Soup for the Soul Enterprises. Audiocassette.

———. 1988. "Developing High Self-Esteem in Yourself and Others." Presentation at the Association for Humanistic Psychology, 26th Annual Meeting, Washington, DC, July.

Childers, J. H., Jr. 1989. "Looking at Yourself Through Loving Eyes." *Elementary School Guidance and Counseling* 23: 204–9.

Childre, D., and D. Rozman. 2003. *Transforming Anger: The HeartMath Solution for Letting Go of Rage, Frustration, and Irritation*. Oakland, CA: New Harbinger.

———. 2005. *Transforming Stress: The HeartMath Solution for Relieving Worry, Fatigue, and Tension*. Oakland, CA: New Harbinger.

Coopersmith, S. 1967. *The Antecedents of Self-Esteem*. San Francisco: Freeman.

Cousins, N. 1983. *The Healing Heart*. New York: Avon.

Davidson, R. 2007. "Changing the Brain by Transforming the Mind: The Impact of Compassion Training on the Neural Systems of Emotion." Paper presented at the Mind and Life Institute Conference, Investigating the Mind, Emory University, Atlanta, GA, October.

De Mello, A. 1990. *Taking Flight: A Book of Story Meditations*. New York: Image Books.

Diener, E. 1984. "Subjective Well-Being." *Psychological Bulletin* 95: 542–75.

Durrant, G. D. 1980. *Someone Special Starring Everyone*. Salt Lake City, UT: Bookcraft Recordings. Audiocassettes.

Enright, R. D. 2001. *Forgiveness Is a Choice: A Step-by-Step Process for Resolving Anger and Restoring Hope*. Washington, DC: American Psychological Association.

———. 2012. *The Forgiving Life: A Pathway to Overcoming Resentment and Creating a Legacy of Love*. Washington, DC: American Psychological Association.

Frankl, V. 1978. *The Unheard Cry for Meaning*. New York: Simon and Schuster.

Fredrickson, B. L., M. A. Cohn, K. A. Coffey, J. Pek, and S. M. Finkel. 2008. "Open Hearts Build Lives: Positive Emotions, Induced Through Meditation, Build Consequential Personal Resources." *Journal of Personality and Social Psychology* 95: 1045–62.

Gallup Organization. 1992. *Newsweek*, February 17.

Gallwey, W. T. 1974. *The Inner Game of Tennis*. New York: Random House.

Gauthier, J., D. Pellerin, and P. Renaud. 1983. "The Enhancement of Self-Esteem: A Comparison of Two Cognitive Strategies." *Cognitive Therapy and Research* 7: 389–98.

Greene, B. 1990. "Love Finds a Way." *Chicago Tribune*, March 11.

Hafen, B. 1989. *The Broken Heart*. Salt Lake City, UT: Deseret Book.

Howard, C. A. 1992. Individual Potential Seminars, West, TX, August.

Hunt, D. S., ed. 1987. *Love: A Fruit Always in Season*. Bedford, NH: Ignatius Press.

Hutcherson, C. A., E. M. Seppala, and J. J. Gross. 2008. "Loving-Kindness Meditation Increases Social Connectedness." *Emotion* 8: 720–4.

Kipfer, B. A. 1990. *14,000 Things to Be Happy About*. New York: Workman Publishing.

Lazarus, A. A. 1984. "Multimodal Therapy." In *Current Psychotherapies*, 3rd ed., edited by R. J. Corsini. Itasca, IL: Peacock.

Leman, K., and R. Carlson. 1989. *Unlocking the Secrets of Your Childhood Memories*. Nashville: Thomas Nelson.

Levin, P. 1988. *Cycles of Power*. Deerfield Beach, FL: Health Communications, Inc.

Lewinsohn, P. M., R. F. Munoz, M. A. Youngren, and A. M. Zeiss. 1986. *Control Your Depression*. New York: Prentice Hall.

Linville, P. W. 1987. "Self-Complexity as a Cognitive Buffer Against Stress-Related Illness and Depression." *Journal of Personality and Social Psychology* 52: 663–76.

Lowry, R. J., ed. 1973. *Dominance, Self-Esteem, Self-Actualization: Germinal Papers of A. H. Maslow.* Monterey, CA: Brooks/Cole.

Maslow, A. 1968. *Toward a Psychology of Being.* 2nd ed. New York: Van Nostrand Reinhold.

Maxwell, N. A. 1976. "Notwithstanding My Weakness." *Ensign,* November. http://www.deseret news.com/article/705384602/Notwithstanding-My-Weakness———Nov-1976-Ensign.html ?pg=all.

Mecca, A., N. Smelser, and J. Vasconcellos. 1989. *The Social Importance of Self-Esteem.* Berkeley: University of California Press.

Meichenbaum, D. 1985. *Stress Inoculation Training.* New York: Pergamon.

Michelotti, J. 1991. "My Most Unforgettable Character." *Reader's Digest,* April, 79–83.

Montegu, A. 1988. "Growing Young: The Functions of Laughter and Play." Paper presented at the Power of Laughter and Play Conference, Toronto, Canada, September.

National Geographic Society. 1986. *The Incredible Machine.* Washington, DC: National Geographic Society.

Neff, K. 2011. *Self-Compassion: The Proven Power of Being Kind to Yourself.* New York: William Morrow.

Neff, K. N. D. Self-Compassion. http://www.self-compassion.org.

Nelson, R. M. 1988. *The Power Within Us.* Salt Lake City, UT: Deseret Book.

Nouwen, H. J. M. 1989. *Lifesigns: Intimacy, Fecundity, and Ecstasy in Christian Perspective.* New York: Image Books.

Office of Disease Prevention and Health Promotion. *2015–2020 Dietary Guidelines for Americans.* US Department of Health and Human Services. http://health.gov/dietaryguide lines/2015/guidelines/

Patinkin, M. 1991. "Little Things That Make Life Worth Living." *Providence Journal-Bulletin,* April 24.

Pennebaker, J. W. 1997. *Opening Up: The Healing Power of Expressing Emotion.* New York: Guilford Press.

Pennebaker, J. W., and J. F. Evans. 2014. *Expressive Writing: Words That Heal.* Enumclaw, WA: Idyll Arbor, Inc.

Pepping, C. A., P. J. Davis, and A. O'Donovan. 2016. "Mindfulness for Cultivating Self-Esteem." In *Mindfulness and Buddhist-Derived Approaches in Mental Health and Addiction,* Advances in Mental Health and Addiction Series, edited by E. Y. Shonin, W. van Gordon, and M. D. Griffiths. Basel, Switzerland: Springer International.

Pepping, C. A., A. O'Donovan, and P. J. Davis. 2013. "The Positive Effects of Mindfulness on Self-Esteem." *Journal of Positive Psychology* 8: 376–86. doi: 10.1080/17439760.2013.807353.

Peterson, C., M. Seligman, and G. Vaillant. 1988. "Pessimistic Explanatory Style as a Risk Factor for Physical Illness: A Thirty-Five-Year Longitudinal Study." *Journal of Personality and Social Psychology* 55: 23–27.

Petrie, A., and J. Petrie. 1986. *Mother Teresa*. San Francisco, CA: Dorason Corporation. DVD.

Piburn, S., ed. 1993. *The Dalai Lama a Policy of Kindness: An Anthology of Writings by and about the Dalai Lama/Winner of the Nobel Peace Prize*. Ithaca, NY: Snow Lion Publications.

Pippert, R. M. 1999. *Out of the Salt Shaker and into the World: Evangelism As a Way of Life*. Downers Grove, IL: Intervarsity Press.

Ratcliff, J. D. 1967–74. "I Am Joe's…" series. *Reader's Digest*.

Richards, S. L. 1955. *Where Is Wisdom? Addresses of President Stephen L. Richards*. Salt Lake City, UT: Deseret Book.

Rogers, F. M. 1970. *It's You I Like*. Pittsburgh, PA: Fred M. Rogers and Family Communications, Inc.

Rorty, R. 1991. "Heidegger, Kundera, and Dickens." In *Essays on Heidegger and Others*. New York: Cambridge University Press.

Saad, Lydia. 2014. "The '40-Hour' Workweek Is Actually Longer—by Seven Hours." Gallup, August 29. Available at http://www.gallup.com/poll/175286/hour-workweek-actually-longer?-seven-hours.aspx?g_source=average%20hours%20worked&g_medium=search&g_campaign=tiles).

Salzberg, S. 1995. *Lovingkindness: The Revolutionary Art of Happiness*. Boston: Shambhala.

Schab, L. M. 2013. *The Self-Esteem Workbook for Teens*. Oakland, CA: Instant Help Books.

Schiraldi, G. R., and S. L. Brown. 2001. "Primary Prevention for Mental Health: Results of an Exploratory Cognitive-Behavioral College Course." *Journal for Primary Prevention* 22: 55–67.

Schlossberg, L., and G. D. Zuidema. 1997. *The Johns Hopkins Atlas of Human Functional Anatomy*. 4th ed. Baltimore: Johns Hopkins University Press.

Schor, J. 1991. "Workers of the World, Unwind." *Technology Review*, November/December, 25–32.

Seuss, Dr. 1990. *Oh, the Places You'll Go!* New York: Random House.

Shahar, B., O. Szsepsenwol, S. Zilcha-Mano, N. Haim, O. Zamir, S. Levi-Yeshuvi, and N. Levit-Binnun. 2015. "A Wait-List Randomized Controlled Trial of Loving-Kindness Meditation Program for Self-Criticism." *Clinical Psychology and Psychotherapy* 22: 346–56. doi: 10.1002/cpp.1893.

Sharapan, H. 1992. Associate Producer, Family Communications, Inc., Pittsburgh, PA. Personal communication, August 20.

Sonstroem, R. J. 1984. "Exercise and Self-Esteem." In *Exercise and Sports Sciences Reviews*, vol. 12, edited by R. L. Terjung. Lexington, MA: The Collamore Press.

Tamarin, A., ed. 1969. *Benjamin Franklin: An Autobiographical Portrait*. London: MacMillan.

Thayer, R. E. 1989. *The Biopsychology of Mood and Arousal*. New York: Oxford University Press.

Worden, J. W. 1982. *Grief Counseling and Grief Therapy: A Handbook for the Mental Health Practitioner*. New York: Springer.

243

Glenn R. Schiraldi, PhD, has served on the stress management faculties at the Pentagon, the International Critical Incident Stress Foundation, and the University of Maryland, where he received the Outstanding Teaching Award, as well as other teaching and service awards. His books on stress-related topics have been translated into fifteen languages. Schiraldi's writing has been recognized by various scholarly and popular sources, including *The Washington Post*, the *American Journal of Health Promotion*, the *Mind/Body Health Review*, and the *International Stress and Tension Control Society Newsletter*. He has trained laypersons and clinicians around the world on various aspects of resilience and trauma, with the goal of optimizing mental health and performance while preventing and promoting recovery from stress-related conditions. His skills-based mind/body courses at the University of Maryland have been found to improve resilience, self-esteem, optimism, happiness, and curiosity, and reduce depression, anxiety, and anger.

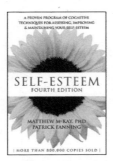

Register your **new harbinger** titles for additional benefits!

When you register your **new harbinger** title—purchased in any format, from any source—you get access to benefits like the following:

- Downloadable accessories like printable worksheets and extra content

- Instructional videos and audio files

- Information about updates, corrections, and new editions

Not every title has accessories, but we're adding new material all the time.

Access free accessories in 3 easy steps:

1. Sign in at NewHarbinger.com (or **register** to create an account).

2. Click on **register a book**. Search for your title and click the **register** button when it appears.

3. Click on the **book cover or title** to go to its details page. Click on **accessories** to view and access files.

That's all there is to it!

If you need help, visit:

NewHarbinger.com/accessories

new harbinger
CELEBRATING
40 YEARS